P9-AEV-952

Home Economics
SHOW-HOW AND SHOWMANSHIP
WITH ACCENT ON VISUALS

HOME ECONOMICS

Show-How and

WRITTEN BY **GENEVIEVE CALLAHA**

ART BY ROBERT COOMBER. PUBLISHED BY T

Showmanship

WITH ACCENT ON VISUALS

AND **LOU RICHARDSON**

IOWA STATE UNIVERSITY PRESS
AMES, IOWA, 1966

Authors

GENEVIEVE CALLAHAN serves as home economics consultant to such business firms and associations as California and Hawaiian Sugar Corporation, Nut Tree Restaurant, and California Lima Bean Advisory Board. She has been an associate editor of *Better Homes and Gardens*; co-editor (with L.R.) of *Sunset Magazine*; and a consistent contributor to a number of home-centered magazines. A graduate of Iowa State University in Home Economics and Journalism, she is a member of Omicron Nu and Theta Sigma Phi, and is active in the Home Economics in Business section of the American Home Economics Association.

LOU RICHARDSON began her editorial career by writing for teachers' magazines while teaching third grade in an Iowa school. This avocation soon led her into editorial work as assistant to the editor of *Better Homes and Gardens*. Next came several years of co-editorship of *Sunset Magazine* with G.A.C. On leaving *Sunset* she contributed regularly to national magazines, while collaborating with G.A.C. in planning and producing materials for advertisers. She is an associate member of Theta Sigma Phi and is an honorary member of the California Home Economics Association.

Stock # 1425

First edition, 1966

Second printing, 1967

Third printing, 1967

Library of Congress Catalog Card Number: 66–14369

Introduction

ABOUT THIS BOOK AND HOW WE CAME TO WRITE IT

As you well know, the problems of communicating clearly with other persons can be complicated and confusing indeed. This is especially true of Home Economics Communications, which abounds in such indefinite expressions as creative thinking, topic-sentence writing, visual presentation, pictorial phraseology, and home economics showmanship.

In this book we have tried to take those vague terms apart and get at the heart of their meanings. To show how to generate creativity, how to figure out and use a topic sentence, how to make the most of visuals, and how to develop showmanship.

Two questions to ask of any book of information: (1) Is there a need for such a book? (2) Does it activate interest in the minds of those who read it?

Like communications itself, this is a many-sided book with many ramifications. Here is presented the composite thinking of many home economists in all branches of the profession and in all parts of the country. Most of the ideas offered have been gathered or developed over a number of years through personal discussions and group meetings such as our Workshops in Home Economics Communications. In addition, we naturally have included ideas and convictions of our own.

As you read, we ask you to keep in mind these two facts:

1. This is an *Idea Book*, not a home economics text. The suggestions given are for you to adapt, change, improve according to your own problems, rather than take too literally. They are in a sense, "patterns"—and idea patterns, like dress patterns, must usually be altered to fit the individual's needs.
2. This book is a companion to our *How To Write for Homemakers.** That volume went into the fundamentals of writing for both printed and oral presentations. This one has to do with unusual yet practical ways of bringing factual homemaking information to life.

Actually, the thought of doing a book on dramatizing home-centered information had been bouncing about in our minds for some time. But it took a whiff of mountain air to send us to the typewriter. This is how it happened.

In the fall of 1964, Dr. Marilyn J. Horn, Associate Director, School of Home Economics, University of Nevada, invited us to conduct an all-day meeting on Communications during the Annual Conference of University and Extension Service staffs. Those participating were the home agents of the state of Nevada, the University Home Economics faculty, and interested students. With that specific audience in mind we planned what we thought would be a helpful and interesting program.

The opening presentation went well enough. But when we turned to the blackboard and began

* Iowa State University Press, 1962.

to talk with the chalk, the meeting really came to life.

"This is what we need," called out one H.D.A. "Give us more! More ideas for visuals that we can develop to fit our own local problems!" And between us all, a number of original solutions to baffling questions were worked out.

On the plane back to San Francisco that evening, one of us remarked, "Judging by the reactions today, there is need for the kind of book we have talked about doing." So on January 1, 1965, we got under way. Now, in 1966, the finished product is in your hands.

We trust that in these pages you will discover not only a great deal of usable information but bits of inspiration, too. If you do find the book helpful, we hope you will recommend it to young professional home economists coming along. Whatever their field of work, they will be looking for ideas and inspiration, and the encouragement to create new patterns of thinking and doing.

GENEVIEVE CALLAHAN
LOU RICHARDSON

San Francisco, California
May, 1966

BULLETIN BOARD OF *Contents*

Home Economics
SHOW-HOW AND SHOWMANSHIP
WITH ACCENT ON VISUALS

1.

Home Economics Showmanship

WHY IT IS NEEDED

It is comparatively simple for a home economist in any branch of the profession to appeal to the reason and influence the thinking of dedicated homemakers, or of eager-to-learn students who are working for degrees in home economics. The big problem lies in trying to interest—and thereby influence—those millions of homemakers and future homemakers who are only casually concerned with the arts and skills of homemaking.

If such groups are to be reached, there must be a hidden ingredient put into every lesson plan, every piece of writing, every photograph, every platform presentation—a certain "something" that attracts attention and stirs the mind. That intangible something is *showmanship*. A special kind of showmanship that turns homemaking into one of the lively arts, while still stressing what is of enduring value.

Showmanship is what makes an audience sit up and take notice, then sit back and take notes.

Such showmanship is a step beyond the show-and-tell technique of presenting information. But it does not imply putting on an act, nor seeking to entertain. It means, literally, bringing basic facts to life in a way that will make them remembered.

Certainly showmanship is as good and honest a word as leadership, sponsorship, and statesmanship. Even so, you may prefer the word "dramatize" to "showmanship." Or you may choose to speak of giving greater visibility to your presentation. Terminology in this case is not important. The question is how to develop and strengthen that much-needed quality.

CREATIVITY

Most creative thinkers start by sensing that a fresh approach is needed, then use all of their senses—especially common sense—to put the ideas in orbit.

START WITH FRESH THINKING

The place to start, it would seem, is to forget temporarily the it-has-always-been-done-this-way approach. Using your mind as an X-ray, take a deep penetrating look at each subject or problem or lesson plan or assignment. In other words, think fresh! For one example of what fresh thinking can bring about, consider what happened to Mrs. Homemaker's sheets.

For many years everyone took it for granted that sheets were white, that they came in three or four standard sizes and in varying grades of cotton. Then someone said, "Why must sheets be white? Why not yellow or blue or pink or green to go with the decor of the room? Why not flower-patterned or striped? Or contrasting trim on a plain color? Why not make them up in crib size, cot size, queen size, and king size, as well as in single and double widths?"

Daring without depth is dangerous . . . depth without daring is likely to be dull. But put daring and depth together and you have dramatization in its highest form.

Others asked, "Why not contour sheets? Why not sheets made of nylon or other fabric that requires no ironing? Why not an electric sheet?" Because someone refused to accept the fact that sheets were sheets and would always remain the same, today's Mrs. H. at a "White Sale" has a delightful variety from which to choose.

Note, however, that white sheets were not

eliminated nor made less usable or practical—quite the contrary. They were modernized and glamorized to appeal to Mrs. H.'s taste.

And so it is in presenting home-centered information. You can always adapt it, style it, to fit it into today's patterns of living, without altering important basic principles.

Your sincere enthusiasm is highly contagious. An epidemic of it can work wonders in communications.

GOING ON FROM THERE

Figuring out a fresh and worthwhile idea is the first step in developing showmanship. And it is a big one. Then comes the problem of communicating that idea to your particular audience of present or future homemakers. To do that you must use spoken or written words, plus whatever visuals will be most helpful in giving life and meaning to your presentation.

Every showman is trying to show something—an object, a stunt, an idea. In a presentation, figure out what you want to show or prove. Then make sure that you put it over. Never confuse true showmanship with what is known as "show business." The two have little or nothing in common.

The idea itself will go a long way toward suggesting its own visuals. Having a hunch for a different type of demonstration is sure to send you scurrying to round up dramatic props and accessories. Thinking up a new twist to an old lesson plan starts you searching through files of pictures and piles of magazines for illustrative material to put on the bulletin board or project onto a screen. Developing a new recipe for newspaper release prompts thinking up a surprising title and planning a dramatic photograph. And in all such instances you work up an enthusiasm which in turn is transferred to your audience or your readers.

AUTHORS' NOTE

Write your own personal notes and observations in these marginal areas. You will then have an Idea Book with two points of view—yours and ours.

WHEN YOU WRITE

Generally speaking, it is easier to put enthusiasm and drama into platform presentations than it is to inject them into writing. Even with a sparkling idea you may become self-conscious when you try to put it into written or printed words. If that is your worry, try this: Forget about using words-that-sound-like-you-think-writing-should-sound. Search your mind for words and expressions that will make pictures—"mental visuals"—in the minds of your readers; then write directly to those readers as if you were talking to them. When you do that, your writing sounds informal and natural. And, as every good actor knows, naturalness is necessary to good showmanship.

One of the first steps in writing or speaking is to establish a mood. In presenting practical information, the dominant mood should be one of helpfulness.

WHY SHOWMANSHIP IS NEEDED

Why all this emphasis on showmanship in home economics communications? The answer is *Competition*. You who teach—especially at the secondary level—are competing for the attention of students whose minds are full of a number of things besides homemaking! You who are concerned with business are competing not only for the time and attention of the homemaker, but for part of her dollar, too. Even home economics itself is competing with other professions, trying to interest girls in taking up careers in home economics rather than in some other field. The only way you can meet such competition is to show that homemaking and home-centered careers can be exciting and worthwhile. And you certainly need to use showmanship if you are going to do that. ●

ASK ONE WHO KNOWS

You simply have to put everything you have into what you are doing if you hope to get across your ideas. Ask any professional person or businessman.

According to Webster's New Collegiate Dictionary, a showman is one who "has a sense or knack for dramatization or visual effectiveness." If you present your material with dramatic effectiveness, you are using showmanship. In doing this you will use visuals—either tangible or mental—so a look at the chapter that follows is in order.

2.

MAKING THE BEST USE OF *Visual Aids*

MANY words and phrases are taken for granted. Used over and over without thinking, they become fixtures in the mind and, like all fixtures, need occasional checkups. For example, the word "Visual" or "Visual Aid." What does the term mean to you?

If you are a teacher, a visual aid is something very real; the words bring to mind an instant picture. If you are a nonteacher, the image is likely to be blurred. You may even say, without thinking, "A visual aid is a filmstrip or something of the sort that is used in the classroom."

But visual aids are for everyone who communicates ideas and information. Certainly they are for you if, in your work, you hope to get across facts or helps or inspirations to your audience.

Visual aids, like flashlights, light up facts at hand and encourage one to explore new paths of learning.

What is needed is expanded thinking. To look at visuals as they are and can become. And how they can be made to emphasize and dramatize home-centered information. Audio-Visual Departments of schools and extension services are constantly and consistently at work doing just that for all types of subject matter. But some of the exploring and thinking is your responsibility, too. Even the most up-to-date and helpful visual equipment cannot do the job alone. You must use it in ways that will best fit your particular group.

In the pentagon figure shown on page 9, the five sides represent five types of visual aids used in interpreting home economics information. They are *Actual Objects; Wall Displays* (as posters, bulletin boards, and the like); *Free-Hand Graphics* (such as you do on chalk board or writing roll); *Photographs* (including film projections); and *Mental Visualizations* (in which you use pictorial words to create pictures in the minds of your listeners).

WHICH VISUALS ARE MOST EFFECTIVE?

One authority lists these:

1. Actual objects—most valuable of all visuals
2. Models and miniatures
3. Active displays put together before the audience—as writing on chalk board or writing roll of a projector
4. Static displays such as charts, photographs, or films

HOW IT WORKS OUT

When you use one or another of those aids, even in a run-of-the-ordinary or unimaginative way, you show some degree of showmanship. But why settle for anything short of a top performance? Look to the symbols. See how easy it is to stretch that pentagon into a star by reaching out in every direction.

For example, in discussing tableware and how to use it, you show place settings. You demonstrate how to hold knife and fork in cutting meat. You are using actual objects as visuals. If, however, on some future field trip, you arrange to have your students visit a well-managed restaurant to see how tables are arranged and how the workers perform their tasks, you have stretched that visual to further dimension.

THE PERSONAL TOUCH

In all visual presentations, personal comments loom large. Often it is the asides that are remembered long after the slick presentation has slipped through the mind of the viewer-listener.

Or you are a business home economist working with textiles—specifically knits. You want to produce a visual that plays up in one picture several smart and interesting ways to wear sweaters. A photograph illustrating so many ideas would be too confusing, therefore out of the question. So you decide on a simple art treatment showing in

From Show-How to SHOWMANSHIP

BUSINESS VISUALS

One specialist says, "Most firms prefer a series of 22″x28″ easel cards to the flip chart." Why? Because most sales presentations are brief, thus requiring only a few cards. (Flips carry as many as 55 or 60.) He also says, "For main points I like to use inch-high letters with a fairly heavy stroke—and always two colors, if possible."

thumbnail sketches how to push up the sleeves of a sweater to give them a graceful look; how to drape a sweater over one's shoulders; or how to dress up a high-neck sweater with just the right accessories.

This composite picture is your first step in reaching out. Now you go further and have that skeletonlike art done on a 10×10-inch card so that it can go into an opaque projector, or can be copied onto a writing roll for overhead projection, or thumbtacked to a bulletin board, or used as a flash card, or reproduced in a publication. When you do this, you have extended one side of that "pentagon" to form a point of the star.

And so it is with every type of visual aid suggested by that pentagon. All will be discussed in detail in the chapters that follow.

Further Thinking

In considering the star approach, think of yourself not only as reaching out for new dimensions for your visuals, but also as reaching out to your audience, making every individual in it see and feel and understand what you are showing and talking about. Remember that the effectiveness of all visuals lies, first of all, in visualizing the audience and figuring out what those homemakers and future homemakers would like to see and hear about.

VISUAL RECIPE FILE

Some home economists simplify and amplify their recipe files by laying a group of related recipe cards, clippings, illustrations, etc. on an 8″ x 11″ sheet of paper, and putting it through the office copying machine. Such copies take up minimum space in the file, are easy to handle and to cross-reference.

One factor often overlooked in discussing visual aids is this: *A well-conceived visual is one that gets down to the heart of the subject matter and brings an idea or fact instantly to life with a minimum of words.* Once the visual is shown, it is, of course, amplified and elaborated, but the essence of thought must be in that visual itself. It is as simple—and as difficult—as that.

Points To Remember

- Visuals have uses and possibilities not yet dreamed of. And they are certainly not confined to the classroom.

- Choose visuals carefully. The fact that a specific wall chart is called a "visual aid" does not necessarily imply that it is right for your audience.

- Visuals must always be thought of as "aids." They cannot be expected to carry the load of teaching.

- Along with ready-to-use visuals, there should be plenty of originals—the ones you figure out for yourself to fit your specific audience. Plenty of "mental visuals," too, in which you use active, pictorial words to create mental pictures.

- Be genuinely enthusiastic in using visuals. An audience is quick to sense the difference.

- Above all, keep in mind that visuals call for showmanship. In preparing or presenting them, think of yourself as using a special kind of showmanship, not merely teaching with the aid of visual material. Practice stretching your imagination in all directions, looking for fresh ideas, new wordage, new ways of doing. Reach out to your audience and beam your message to every individual in it. When you are able to do this, you should take a bow. For you have, indeed, become a star performer, and you and your message will be remembered.

And now to a group of pictorials that will remind you of some of the equipment and materials that can be used to give dimension and visibility to your presentations.

PARADOX

With all of the emphasis on visual aids, why are so many picture-making words being replaced by general terms? This is something to watch when writing for general publication. To illustrate:

If a magazine article is titled, "Camping in the High Sierra," an instant picture clicks in one's mind. If it says, "Vacationing in the Mountains," the mental picture is less sharp. If it says, "Advantages of Recreation"—no picture!

By the same reasoning, the words "marketing," "cooking," or "baking" create clear pictures in the minds of homemakers. The general term "Food Preparation" suggests pictures to home economists, but not always to Mrs. H.

Keep up-to-date with

Overhead projectors—short cut to good viewing

You who make use of visuals will sense immediately that the devices pictured here are merely a sampling of the many aids that are, or eventually will be, available: dioramas showing kitchens of other ages and other countries . . . life-sized cardboard dolls on which to thumbtack garments . . . involved wheels and mobiles for meal-planning lessons . . . tests put on filmstrips that help the teacher to determine the student's rate of thinking. The list constantly grows longer.

How do you keep in step with visual equipment? If you are a teacher, such information will probably be brought to your attention by your supervisor or your audio-visual department. If you are in extension work, you will be working with others to explore new possibilities. (Televised programs, for example.) If you are a business home economist,

Transparencies

Film Strips

Opaque projectors have many uses

Equipment and Materials

The textured look with screen squares

your awareness of such innovations will be sharpened by the need to keep ahead of your competitors; your inquiring, creative mind will provide ideas for adaptations.

The idea for the illustration at upper right, for example, came as a result of browsing around an art supply store. Adhesive-backed papers used in making charts prompted one home economist to experiment—a few quick snips with the scissors turned out a "dress" that could be literally ironed onto cardboard to make a display card calling attention to a store style show.

All ideas and equipment for visual presentations have come about because of someone's vision. When you get on the beam of such thinking, you will see limitless possibilities that are yours for the using.

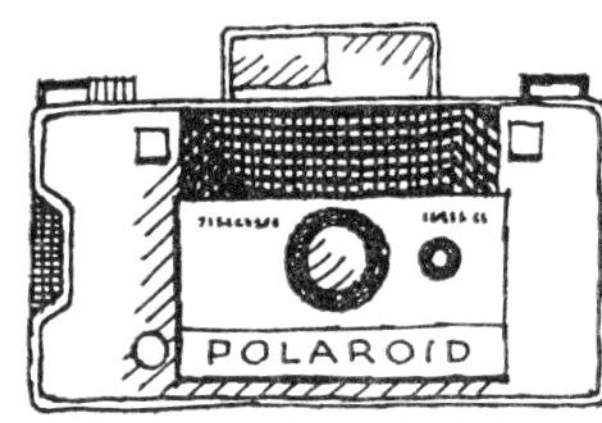

Land Cameras

Spot-lights

Sound Recorders

SIZE OF GROUP

In a small group, actual objects can be passed from one to another; all present can see a chalkboard graphic. But for a large group in a large room, projected visuals are the answer. They are part of our mechanical production world.

Use your "third" eye to look into the minds of your students or homemakers. Use it also to see new possibilities in all visual aids. Then watch audience reaction.

WHAT ABOUT TELE-VISUALS?

As you are well aware, one visual that affects the life of every student and homemaker is television. You may or may not have closed-circuit viewing in your building. You may or may not be actively concerned with what is spoken of as "Educational Television." You may or may not see much in commercial programs or documentaries that relates to your classroom or platform presentations in homemaking. However, when you mention something you have seen on television, you establish a bond with your audience, because, in a sense, you have put yourself on its wavelength. Often such a bond is of greater importance than the single thought you are trying to teach or show at the moment.

Perhaps, in the final analysis, part of the strength of visual teaching lies in the fact that teacher and student are seeing things together. A community of interest and understanding is developed which has far-reaching effects for all concerned. ●

3.

Styling Foods — WHERE TO START AND WHEN TO STOP

IN TODAY'S scheme of things it is not enough to be able to prepare foods and to plan meals. You need to know how to style them—show them off to best advantage. In other words, you must use showmanship. This is especially important in photographing or displaying food. If you are not quite sure where and how to start doing this, just keep in mind that *food styling (like style in dress) is simply an expression of good taste, plus an awareness of what is smart and appropriate.* Then work to develop that awareness.

There is all the difference in the world between styling food and merely making it look fancy.

HOW IT WORKS OUT

Situation. You are a business home economist working for an equipment company, planning a demonstration that is to feature small electrical appliances. Seeing a shiny pizza pan in a hardware store starts you wondering about a new type of dessert pizza—perhaps chocolate cream filling with crushed almonds. You say to yourself, "I could have the rich pastry done in advance and show baking it in our new oven. I could use the

Ideas ***are originated*** *in* ***answer to*** *a* ***real*** *need.* (Just another way of expressing the old saying, "Necessity is the mother of invention.")

small mixer to whip up the filling. And I could show pulverizing the blanched almonds in the blender and adding them to the whipped cream."

When you do all of these and more, you have styled your demonstration!

Situation. Your job is to work out recipe releases to send to food editors. In browsing through an old cookbook, you come across a recipe for old-fashioned clotted cream. It prompts you to try a modern version by whipping together cream cheese and sour cream. You like the way it comes out, and decide to use it for a topping for canned peaches. Result: an almost new recipe for something that you call "Cling Peach Crisp with New Creamy Topping." And it came about because you were aware of the possibilities in that old-time recipe.

HOLIDAY IDEA

Make corsages of watercress, tying each with plastic ribbon. Just before serving time, stack them carefully on an elevated plate or basket to make a "Christmas tree" for the buffet table. Each guest puts one of the bunches on his or her dinner plate for the "salad."

Situation. You are a teacher concerned with the Chinese dinner your students are planning as part of a series of "Foods Around the World." Since the girls intend to serve fortune cookies as part of the dessert, you drop the hint that it might be interesting to impale the cookies on bamboo sticks of various lengths, and stand them in a tall glass for the centerpiece. Later you add that it might be fun to try using melted chocolate to paint faces or butterfly wings on the cookies. As idea piles upon idea, interest in the dinner grows and students become aware of what can be done to make food more dramatic, more fun.

One California HEIB often puts a smile into her food—as decorating a springtime platter of corned beef with a sprig of wild mustard blossoms.

Situation. In your school it has been the custom to give a Mother's Day Tea each year. But your community has been changing. Many of your students have never heard of a tea, nor seen a tea service. After talking about teas and their expression of hospitality, you suggest that, instead of the traditional long tea table, it might be newer and more interesting to use three tables. One for coffee and one for tea, separated by a longer one for the food. This would make it easy to use whatever coffeepots and teapots were available—and certainly not fancy ones.

Discussion brings out ways of decorating the three tables so that there is uniformity. This might lead to the idea of using two big, round trays—one for the sandwiches, one for the cookies, with a flower arrangement between them. If the girls decide on daffodils (for example), you mention that it might be dramatic to tuck a few heads of the flowers in among the sandwiches and cookies. And before you or your students realize it, you are on your way to new styling for that Mother's Day Tea.

Germs of ideas are everywhere. Reach out for them. But remember, always, that the most effective food styling comes from an awareness of some basic problem and the imagination to solve it in some unusual way.

PLASTIC FOAM

A circle of plastic foam under a white-frosted cake adds height and drama. A square of it standing on edge makes a frosty background for a pitcher of iced drink on a buffet table; an oblong bar of it can hold appetizers on picks, thus making a conversation piece.

BE AWARE OF DESIGN

In all of your efforts to style food—whether to be photographed or displayed or written about or eaten—remember your A.B.C.'s: *A* for Appetite Appeal; *B* for Balance of forms and textures; and *C* for Color Contrasts. Then add *D* for Design, and your production is almost certain to be dramatic.

Never underestimate the importance of design. Learn more about it. Work for sureness with food which is always the mark of the professional. If you are an "old pro," you have achieved that sure touch. If you are a beginner, put down

BE AN ARTIST

When arranging individual plates, proceed as an artist does in planning a painting. Put the largest or the featured item first, then fit in the other elements for best effect and easiest eating.

the following suggestions on your list of Things-I-Need-To-Remember:

• In arranging several foods, as on a dinner plate, turn pork chops or lamb chops at an interesting angle. Serve fried or broiled chicken pretty-side up. Overlap thin slices of meat, as ham or corned beef. Turn prawns or shrimp so that they make an attractive pattern. If the main dish is a casserole mixture, consider using individual casseroles, and break up the top of each one in some interesting way; then round out the plate with something that adds color and texture, and helps to create a pleasing design.

HEIGHT AND DARING

Why do goblets, footed sherbet glasses, elevated cake plates, and the like seem more festive than ordinary tumblers, sauce-dishes, and plates? Because height suggests importance.

Dare to use those tall items dramatically—tiny tomatoes on a bed of parsley in a big beer goblet; a miniature seafood salad in a tall sherbet glass; fruit and cheese on that elevated cake plate.

• Get a feeling of height onto the plate—a baked potato or an artichoke or a lettuce cup of salad or appetizer will do it. Keep in mind that little mounds of formless vegetables can disturb what might otherwise be good design. (Two or three small corn fritters or a half-ear of corn have more character than several spoonfuls of loose kernels. Peas creamed with new potatoes have more plate appeal than peas that roll.) Asparagus, carrots, and zucchini cut on the bias, rather than crosswise, often arrange to better advantage. The seed pattern in cucumbers contributes interesting design.

TRAY COLOR

At least one convalescent hospital uses trays of a different color for each specific type of diet. Saves time and words in giving orders, and brightens mealtime a bit for those captive diners.

• If a salad is to be tossed and served in bowls, tuck in slices of cucumber or wedges of tomato to provide pattern. In plate salads, every individual leaf of lettuce is part of the over-all design. If feasible serve 2-piece desserts—as ice cream and cake; fruit and cheese; fruit compote and cookies. When two items are used, design as well as balance of taste are possible.

All food arranging starts, of course, with preliminary planning; with visualizing in advance just how the food will look when served. If you find it difficult to imagine those finished servings, use paper plates and colored crayons to work out a preview. Since you are planning on paper, you can scribble and erase, or start over on another plate, until you get just the effect you want. The visual below tells the story of what can happen.

CHANGE WITH THE TIMES

Don't be afraid to adapt a table-setting rule to fit a special situation. Most important rule of all is to keep the comfort and pleasure of the diners in first place in your thinking.

Situation. You are a Home Advisor (Home Demonstration Agent) trying to teach plate design as well as meal planning to a group of homemakers. The menu decided upon for a hypothetical buffet supper consists of spaghetti with meat balls; hard rolls; a tossed green salad; fruit; and cold drink or coffee. You pass out paper plates so each can try out her own ideas. When, in their doodling, your homemakers find it difficult to arrange the food attractively on ordinary round plates, you suggest that perhaps paper steak plates (which are shaped like platters) might be a solution. Experimenting with that new idea, the meeting comes to life. Instead of a green salad, the group decides to serve

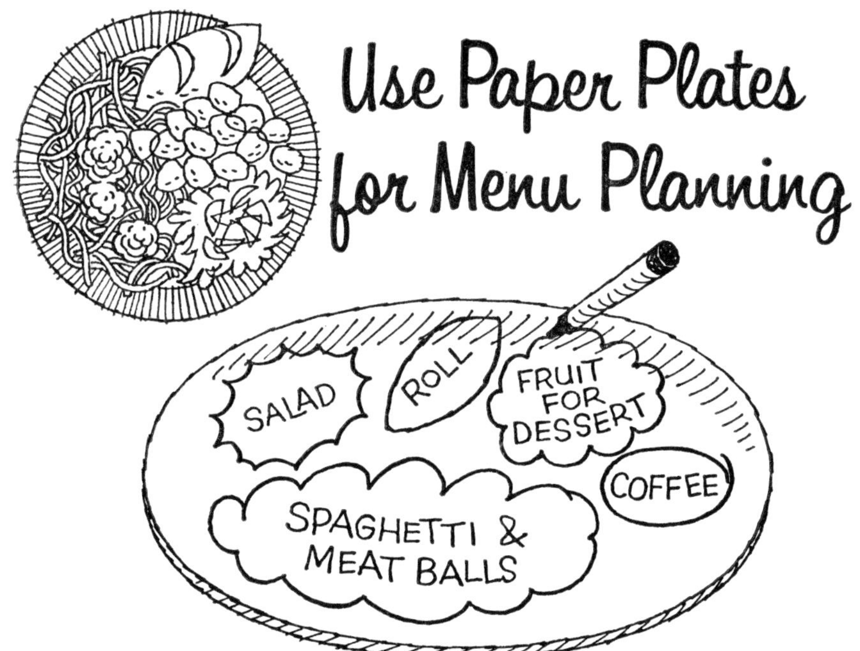

a green bean salad in one lettuce cup, and melon balls in another. And so new ideas develop. Thus, by sensing the real problem and rethinking it, you and the group have styled an all-on-one-plate supper in a fresh, attractive, yet sensible way. And made the meeting fun.

BE AWARE OF WHEN TO STOP

Knowing where and how to start in styling food is only half the problem; the other half lies in knowing where and when to stop! In realizing that showmanship can—and sometimes does—turn into "show*off*manship." For example, a salad tossed at table can be a conversation piece, or a cliché. The mere fact that the waiter in a popular restaurant pours salad dressing with a flourish from a height of two or three feet or grinds pepper in a 15-inch-tall pepper mill does not, in itself, represent salad sophistication. A simpler salad often says it better.

GARNISH

Don't use parsley tentatively. Make it into a "corsage" and place it on the platter emphatically.

On occasion an overenthusiastic stylist may turn out a cake that is literally out of this world, in that it is too far out to be cut or served gracefully. An inexperienced one may overprettify a photographic setup to the point that it looks fussy rather than dramatic. An art director may insist upon a towering molded salad that would be destined to doom if it were ever to be served. In arranging a tray of appetizers (either in real life or in a picture) one sometimes is tempted to make too rigid a pattern. In reaching out for a new angle or a new twist to food, there can be the danger of reaching beyond what is reasonable.

PANCAKE STYLING

Can you remember when pancakes were just pancakes? Look at them now! One national chain of Pancake Houses lists 18 different kinds—each distinctively styled. Everything from Midwest Buckwheats to the African Banana. Proving that food styling is big business!

Best answer, always, in styling food is to think big—looking here, there, everywhere, and especially within your own mind, for those germs of fresh ideas—and then bring the ideas down to practicality and workability. Ask yourself: Am I using true food showmanship, or am I just showing off? Am I teaching students to think creatively, or merely cramming their minds with my own ideas? Am I helping homemakers to serve really good food in imaginative ways, or am I encouraging them to go fancy without regard to what might be called basic styling?

All of this needs to be considered when you are working to put showmanship and style into the serving of food. For notes on putting showmanship into the writing of recipes, see Chapter 6 of the book *How To Write for Homemakers*, Iowa State University Press, Ames, 1962. ●

Food historians say that all recipes are descended from about a dozen basic ones. Little lesson in humility worth noting: All of these recipes were developed ages ago, before there was such a person as a home economist! Note, however, that the field is wide open for adapting and styling those originals!

4. ADDING SPARKLE TO *Nutrition* INFORMATION

SOME OF YOU may reason—and rightly—that, since good nutrition is of vital importance to every individual, it should not be necessary to dramatize the subject matter. You do know that in some instances and for some groups, dramatization is needed. The question is, why is it so difficult to bring nutrition facts and information to life, with or without the use of visual aids? One reason is a lack of audience participation.

KEEPING THE AUDIENCE BUSY

More persons than you may realize are hungry for helpful information—and inspiration — about nutrition.

At times a lesson or a lecture may be opened up for discussion, but rarely is there an opportunity for the audience to get into the act. High school students, Girl Scouts, 4-H girls, and others of that age group particularly need to do something that makes them feel they have a part in the lesson or meeting. They respond to activities that force them to open their eyes to new and live applications of nutrition information. This idea, for example:

Before the class assembles, write in bold letters on the chalk board a list of foods that might be featured in a cafeteria menu:

Veal Stew with Vegetables
Pot Roast with Gravy
Hot Dogs (2)
Tuna Noodle Casserole
Creamed Eggs with Ham
Lima Bean Soup
Buttered Carrots
Hamburger Sandwich
Chicken Sandwich
Potato Salad
Cabbage Salad
Macaroni Salad
Cottage Cheese
Hard Roll
Corn Bread
Cup Custard
Chocolate Cake
Apple Pie
Gelatin with Fruit Sauce
Ice Cream
Milk

IS IT A TREND?

Breakfast of orange juice, sweet rolls, and milk served in high school cafeterias. Some educators report that it gives students the feeling of being adult, develops responsibility, and teaches social amenities. Nutritionists and mothers are pleased to see the children eat breakfast in any form!

At lesson time hand each girl a sheet of unruled paper, typewriter size. This represents her tray. The idea is to study the menu, then select an imaginary lunch or dinner from those items, drawing and writing them on her "tray," as

QUESTION: Is it possible to use too many visuals?

ANSWER: How many are too many?

Such an activity takes but a few minutes, then you introduce several other exercises in which they may participate. One would be to insert after each item on the chalk board its approximate number of calories, and have each student figure the total number of calories in the meal she has selected. Or quickly analyze two or three of the trays before the class, in order to show which choices were most desirable from the standpoint of good nutrition. Or, add price to each item on the menu, thus giving the class an opportunity to see how much good nutrition can be bought for a specified sum of imaginary money.

Whatever direction the presentation takes, each girl studies the principles of good nutrition in relation to her own personal eating habits and needs and adds to her working knowledge of the subject. Why? Because she is sharing in an activity—not merely sitting and taking notes while the teacher talks.

NUTRITION VISUALS

Home advisors (particularly those working with disadvantaged groups) have found that actual foods make the best visual aids. Example: Teacher holds up a cabbage head, discusses cost; talks about Vitamin C; gives suggestions for cooking, or serving as salad. Offers, perhaps, an extra good recipe for salad dressing.

USING FAMILIAR SYMBOLS

Another way to spark an interest in nutrition is through the use of familiar objects.

The TV Dinner. ("T-V" in this case standing for True Value.) At the beginning of the class period, hold up an aluminum plate which originally held a TV dinner. One with five compartments is good, because it suggests all five food groups. After commenting on the fact that the lesson has to do with a new type of TV dinner, do a chalk-board graphic something like this. (Or do it in advance on cardboard.)

Since every student is familiar with TV dinners, she immediately identifies herself with the visual. The lesson can proceed in any one of a number of directions: For example, have the class work out a menu to fit the plate, choosing items for each group. Or stress the idea of combining the meat group with the cereal group—as spaghetti with meat balls; chicken pot pie; creamed tuna on waffles; or beef stew on rice. In addition to the TV dinner, there might be two 3-section plates—one labeled "True-Value Breakfast" and the other "True-Value Lunch." By looking at the three together, the day's meals are seen and judged at a glance.

Nutrition information, to be most effective, should be administered in small doses. Few students or homemakers can absorb facts in big gulps.

True-Value Dinner

MEAT GROUP
VEGETABLE-FRUIT GROUP
BREAD CEREAL GROUP
OTHER FOODS
MILK GROUP

The Automobile. Another symbol familiar to everyone is the automobile, which makes it a natural to help in dramatizing nutrition information for an audience of any age. For a starter, perhaps you will hold up a toy automobile, or a photograph of a new model sports car, or a Volkswagon advertisement—fitting the choice to your audience.

Let the four wheels of the car represent the four major food groups. You need very few words to get across the idea that if a tire on one wheel

APPEALS

Few persons eat food on the basis of what is "good for them." The approach, "It's good to eat and helps you, too," is generally more acceptable.

goes flat (i.e., if one food group is neglected) the automobile (human body) fails to travel smoothly—may even skid!

Or, in stressing the need for an adequate breakfast, bring out that a man about to take an automobile trip makes sure he has gasoline in the tank before he heads for the freeway. Going without breakfast or settling for just a cup of coffee means starting a fast-moving day without enough "fuel in the tank" to last until lunch time.

STUDENT JUDGING

In one Junior High, the home economics teacher assembled a collection of wall charts and other materials relating to nutrition; asked students to point out the ones that seemed to them most valuable.

TAILORING VISUALS TO FIT THE AUDIENCE

Wise home economics teachers scrutinize all nutrition visuals in advance of showing in order to tailor them to fit her particular group of students. When a poster, for example, gives the milk equivalent of a 1-inch cube of cheese, some groups will need to see the amount of a cube converted into slices—the cheese form most familiar to sandwich makers and sandwich eaters. When a chart speaks of an 8-ounce glass or cup of milk, you may feel the need to go a step further and show an actual glass of milk that size and then relate it to a measuring cup, then to a quart carton of milk.

In charts listing vegetables and fruits that are valuable sources of Vitamin A and Vitamin C, it may be well in some instances to underscore the most familiar varieties to make them stand out. (Some students who are not familiar with collards, cress, artichokes, etc., find such words stumbling blocks.)

When the recommended servings of meat, poultry, and fish are given in ounces, the relation of weight-in-ounces to size or quantity can be more quickly grasped if a postal scale is used to weigh a cooked hamburger patty, or two fried drumsticks, or two weiners. The aim must always be to develop understanding and judgment in students, rather than expect them to memorize figures.

Show-how is the short-cut to explaining information and ideas. Showmanship is the step beyond—the step which makes ideas come through and be remembered.

TAKING ADVANTAGE OF THE UNEXPECTED

If you are a home economist working with adult groups, you know that homemakers respond to case histories and conversation pieces, especially those with an unexpected twist. Examples:

• One Home Advisor speaks of her "V.I.P. Diet Plan." At the beginning of the meeting she announces that, since all homemakers are V.I.P.'s (very important persons), why not a V.I.P. Diet Plan? Translated, the *V* represents Vitamins; the *I* stands for Iron and other minerals; and the *P* is for Protein. The brief discussion which follows the introduction is, in turn, followed by a meal-planning lesson that puts particular attention on Vitamins, Iron and other minerals, and Protein—the dietary necessities which are most likely to run low in the daily food patterns of homemaking women.

• A home economist for a dairy company specializes in what she calls "Sophisticated Nutrition." In her demonstrations she shows how to make Vichyssoise, Cheese Soufflé, Café au lait, and other glamorous-sounding food specialties that call for milk or milk products. Her programs are invariably popular.

SHE ASKED FOR HELP

One teacher asked one of her students to be a "consultant" as to what young people would like to know about good nutrition, and to suggest ways the information might best be presented. Teacher's eyes were opened through that frank discussion.

• One extension home agent is known for her nutrition sessions that are well sprinkled with unusual case histories. In one such meeting she told about the farm mother whose youngsters, always hurrying to catch the school bus, rarely had time to eat breakfast. And how the mother solved the problem by handing each child an apple half and a skillet-browned hot dog in a roll as he went out the door. The discussion that followed was a lively one, packed with pro's and con's and contributions of other ideas. But the unorthodox idea made the audience think. And that was, of course, the aim of the leader.

WORD FRESHENERS

One way to dramatize nutrition facts is to state them in lively language. As when Donald Duck speaks of orange juice as "the pitcher of health."

Other examples of fresh wordage: think slim . . . every calorie counts . . . breads and spreads . . . meat and milk power . . . the lively leafies . . .

DRAMATIZING WRITTEN MATERIAL

What about presenting nutrition information in written form—as in leaflets, releases, and the like which give the reader-audience no opportunity to ask questions or share in any activity? This is an area where writing skill is definitely needed.

Since the subject matter does not lend itself easily to a direct, me-to-you style of writing, you need to take advantage of every device possible to give the impression that you are speaking directly and personally to each one who will read what you have to say. Use short sentences and short paragraphs to make the reading look easy. Substitute simple, easy-to-understand words for technical terms. (If you must use a technical term, define it.) Where possible, illustrate your material with meaningful photographs or charts that not only have a direct connection with the subject, but that are interesting to the readers. Make the most of case histories when this can be done without interrupting the train of thought.

If you are writing to other scientists, such precautions may or may not be important. But when you write for public consumption, put people and their nutrition problems ahead of your own interest in the subject. Unless you can do this, your knowledge of nutrition feeds only the scientific minds of other nutritionists. ●

5. TODAY'S WAYS WITH *Food Demonstrations*

SPEAKING OF WORDS, what about that word *Demonstrations*? It has been a special word in home economics all through the years—a word that suggests show-how based on know-how. Unfortunately, however, in the eyes of the general public, demonstrations have recently come to mean protestations against real or imaginary grievances, or against individuals or forms of government. A marching for or against something.

In view of this, will it eventually become advisable to figure out a new word for demonstrations as they apply to homemaking? It is something to think about. Certainly homemaking demonstrations themselves have been changing since the early days of home economics. And they will continue to change—possibly more in the future than in the past. Look at this audio-visual device in relation to your own job.

Demonstration techniques are changing. Challenge is to change with them, yet hold fast to fundamentals.

As a business home economist, you do not stage the 2-hour cooking schools that were par for the course in the '20's. But you find yourself doing short dramatic demonstrations—live or on film—for special groups of homemakers and for special occasions. You may be faced with planning new types of presentations consisting of static displays that can be explained in brief captions for use in fairs, food shows, and the like, or described in few words on television.

ALL DEMONSTRATIONS

THE INFORMATION AND IDEAS GIVEN IN THIS CHAPTER ARE ADAPTABLE TO DEMONSTRATIONS OF SUBJECT MATTER OTHER THAN FOODS.

If your company brings out a new food product, you may be called upon to introduce it (in a way, "demonstrate" it) to members of the press at a luncheon or dinner. A part of your job may be to set up and demonstrate new product uses for the salesmen in your organization. If you are a young, inexperienced home economist, you may not think of these as demonstrations, but that is exactly what they are.

If you teach foods at any level, you still follow the demonstration method of teaching—you show how and explain techniques. But each year you rethink your approach to fit the changing makeup of the community; the changing times; the changing styles in equipment, foods, and clothing and resulting changes in techniques; and the ever-changing mental timing of your students.

Regardless of changes and trends, however, when you give any demonstration you have to use showmanship—that special kind of showmanship which makes information more meaningful to an audience.

VISUALIZE THE AUDIENCE

In every demonstration the audience sits back and says, in effect, "Well, show us. We're waiting!" And so you do just that—immediately, but not in a show-off way.

In the classroom you know the types of girls you must reach in your teaching. When presenting a live demonstration to a group of homemakers, you can usually sense whether or not your ideas are getting through. If your demonstration is to be filmed, it is more difficult to adapt it to all the various audiences to which it will be offered. Important thing is to keep an open mind, avoiding rigid preconceived ideas as to what will be of highest interest.

Your students, for example, may respond much more quickly to a demonstration of making biscuit-type strawberry shortcake than they would to a routine lesson on biscuit making. Or to a demonstration of preparing deviled eggs for a party rather than of soft- or hard-cooked eggs for breakfast—yet the fundamentals of biscuit making and egg cooking are taught in either case. A discussion of meal planning that starts with dinner or a company brunch is likely to attract more attention than one that begins all too logically with everyday breakfast-getting.

THOSE FIRST FEW MINUTES

Within the first few minutes bring on a spectacular food feature. Talk about it, then show how to put it together. This is not a new device—but it always builds up interest for the acts that are to follow.

At first thought it might seem that a group of young marrieds in a low-income category would welcome a demonstration of "Hillbilly Chili"—a good chili-bean mixture with canned, black-eyed peas added. Seasoned reasoning, however, might tell you that while the girls would like to have such a recipe, they feel a greater need for learning how to make a good main dish for a company dinner—chicken curry, for example.

A California home economist conducting cooking classes for a group of new-in-our-country Mexican girls found that the thing which impressed them most was learning to make radish roses. This to them was a status symbol. Taking this as a cue, the wise home economist swung her series of lessons around to cooking for guests, punctuating each demonstration with plenty of asides as to techniques, nutrition, and how to do things the California way!

NOTE

Tell what you are doing, but don't call all the shots. The audience can see that you are going to the refrigerator without your saying so!

FIGURE OUT NEW IDEAS

There is no yardstick for measuring an audience. Some students and homemakers enjoy hearing about foods as served in other countries (cookies around the world, for example). Others respond to bits of food history, as bread through the

Don't stop with making a salad or casserole or dessert. Show how to serve it and suggest how to build a meal around it. Put flair as well as flavor into what you show.

ages. Some want to learn, some want to be entertained. But almost everyone likes to see a familiar type of recipe approached from a brand-new angle. It is never easy to figure out new twists, but the results are worth the effort. Example:

- You are planning to show a group of Girl Scouts how to make simple drop cookies and are looking for that fresh approach. Noting that the recipe lists 12 ingredients gives you the germ of an idea. There are 12 figures on a clock, so why not call them "Good Time Cookies?" Going on from there, you decide to open the demonstration by holding up a cardboard clock, or you refer the girls to a real clock in the room.

Every audience is a challenge. You need intuition to reach each person.

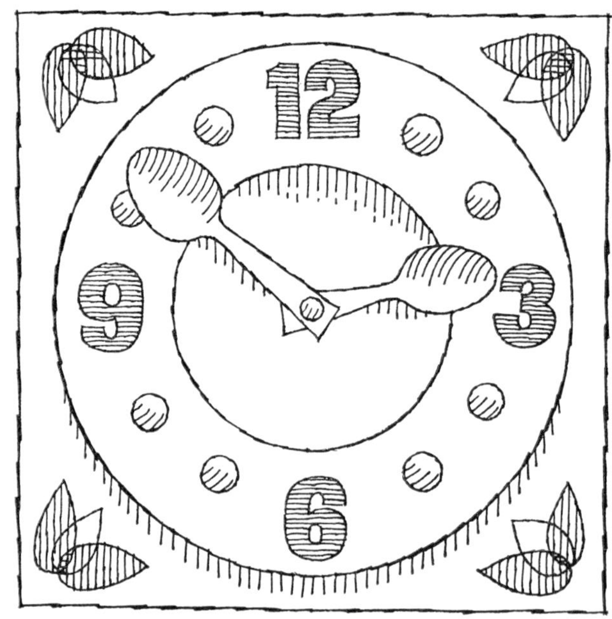

Your running comments bring out thoughts such as these: Recipe calls for 12 ingredients. Using your own two hands, you can put the recipe together in about 12 minutes. (Bring in timer.) In baking, set timer for 12 minutes. (Cookies may take two or three minutes longer, but it's well to look at them when the timer goes off.) Recipe makes 24 (or 48) cookies—twice or 4 times around the clock. Cookies are good any time of day—with a glass of milk; with canned fruit; to go with ice cream, and so on. As you sign off, suggest that looking at a clock at any time is a reminder to make Good Time Cookies.

KEEP IN MIND THAT WORD, "NEWS"

In planning any demonstration, ask yourself, "Does this have news value?" If it has none, figure out where and how news can be injected. Here, again, the problem goes back to the audience. The young homemaker may welcome a demonstration of making a simple but superb veal stew. To her, making a stew is news. But her mother (who has been making stew for years) might respond more enthusiastically to something called *Estofado a la Mexicana*, or Mexican Stew.

A beginning cook may like to learn how to put frosting curlicues on a birthday cake; the more sophisticated (already familiar with frosting making) might prefer a demonstration of *Zabaglione* that uses the yolks of eggs left from a 7-minute frosting. To the inexperienced, making any jam for the first time is new; the experienced find news in a gorgeous cherry-berry jam made with fresh or frozen fruits.

In bringing the news angle into demonstrations, there are three "nevers" to look out for:

1. Never say that something is new or original unless you are absolutely certain that it is.

2. Never leave the impression that something is the "last word"; next week something may come along that makes today's news obsolete.

DRAMA IN SMALL DOSES

If possible, avoid working on a high stage—especially if the group is a small one.

Check the lighting in advance. It is just as important in a demonstration as it is in a stage or screen production.

Get color into the setting in big and little ways—a colorful screen or curtain for a background; a bowl of tomatoes on the table.

Be friendly and informal. And look pretty. You are the actress in this show; act the part.

3. Never give the impression that what you are showing or telling belongs to you alone. It is often better to say, "This was news to me," or, "This seems to be the new way of doing."

OLD SONG

Do you remember the popular song of a few years ago that ended, "You can be better than you are. You could be swinging on a star!"

GET IN THE WHY'S AND WHEREFORE'S

One way to put showmanship into a demonstration is to work in plenty of reasons why. In rolling out pastry, for example, you do explain what you are doing and why. But go a step further and remark that by *not* rolling the pastry clear to the edge, it is easier to pick up and drape into the pan without tearing. If you are using a wire whisk to beat eggs, show the whisk and explain why you are using it instead of the beater. If you are using a marble slab for making fondant, state your reasoning, then go on to suggest that a cold, oven-glass platter is a good substitute for the marble. Old pro's are aware of all this. These reminders are for you who are just starting on your career in home economics.

IDENTIFY! IDENTIFY!

Tie together your action and product with printed or written words. You who teach know the value of using the chalk board to write down points under discussion. You spell out words as students write them in their notebooks. You teach by association. In a platform demonstration, spell out and give meanings of strange words, particularly foreign terms. Hold up lettered identification cards, or flash them on a screen. In static displays, as in presenting new dishes to salesmen, elaborate on those labels. Instead of a card that says merely "Banana Cup Cakes," add something that contributes to the sales possibilities, as, "Banana Cup Cakes—take 1 pound of brown sugar!"

DRAMATIC DECORATION

Make up 3 or 4 dozen nylon net dishcloth balls in an assortment of colors. Pile them high on a tray to make a gay display for your demonstration. Show using one of them—perhaps to wash the beaters of the electric mixer. Suggest other uses such as for washing bathtubs and windows. At meeting's end, toss the balls into the audience!

DEVISE IDEAS FOR AUDIENCE PARTICIPATION

Even though the audience is interested in watching you and listening to you, it likes to get into the act, too. Encourage them. One home economist, showing how to flute pastry, had everyone in the audience fluting a piece of paper between thumb and forefinger as she was doing. Another introduced what she called her "Cool Cooking School" by handing out paper plates on which she had put a few decorative touches. After announcing that these take-home souvenirs were to be used as fans to carry out the theme of the meeting, she suggested using the backs of the plates for note taking. Another always breaks her demonstrations midway with a 5-minute question period, rather than waiting until the end of the meeting. The possibilities for participation are many—use them!

BIRTHDAY TOUCH

Birthdays are big business! How about showing a birthday "fruit cake"—a thick round of peeled watermelon, with candles stuck into it . . . Or an Edam cheese decorated with candles on a tray with grapes and pears . . . Or a big unfrosted angel cake decorated with tiny flags of all nations, rather than with candles.

TIE YOUR PACKAGE NEATLY

How do you end a demonstration? On a high note, always, with a quick recapitulation of what has been done. But do give the feeling that every story of food is a continued story—to be continued in each person's home kitchen.

And whatever your demonstration, keep in mind the Four Freedoms:

1. *Freedom from Unsureness.* Work for a sure touch in everything that you do.
2. *Freedom from Stiffness.* Be informal.
3. *Freedom from Glibness.* Take time to explain important points.
4. *Freedom from Self-centeredness.* Avoid overuse of that pronoun "I"—make it "You!" ●

REMEMBER

Even though you are an authority and must proceed as one, a little humility is appreciated. One rarely thinks of humility as being akin to showmanship. But it is. Ask any showman.

CHAPTERETTE: *Flowery Visuals*

NO DOUBT you have often used flowers in a variety of ways to help in dramatizing home-centered information. But perhaps there are flowery paths you have not yet explored. For example:

ONE FLORAL STYLIST SAYS:

"In a banquet room where there are numerous small tables, elevate the flower arrangements on tall, slender standards. This gives a flowery effect to the entire room, and does not interfere with across-the-table conversation."

• Have you ever decorated the top of a wedding cake with a dramatic arrangement of flowers and ferns, rather than with the ubiquitous "bride and groom"? Then demonstrated how to lift off the flower-decked top layer and set it aside while the bride and groom cut the first slice from the next layer? (Later, the flowers are removed from that top layer which is then wrapped and frozen for the bridal pair to share on their first anniversary—a charming custom of the day.)

• In your food preparation classes you have discussed flower arrangements for tables. But have you shown how attractive it is to use an individual flower in place of other garnish for a salad or dessert plate? Be sure to use flowers from a non-toxic plant; and place the flower head so that it looks up at the diner.

In selecting flowers to be used at night, stay by the whites and yellows. Most blue, pink, and lavender flowers have a tendency to look dull and "washed out" under artificial light.

• Since flowers are things of temporary rather than long-lasting beauty, one should be discreet about using wallpapers of bold floral design—especially if the paper is not likely to be replaced for several seasons. As a home advisor, you have suggested that; but have you, in teaching money management, used flowers to illustrate this point: just as beautiful bouquets are built by artfully putting together a number of individual flowers, so is a family's financial security built by putting together small, seemingly insignificant savings or assets. (Yes, this does take a little longer than arranging a bouquet!) •

6. ACTIVATING *Clothing* IN THE CLASSROOM

EVERYTHING about courses in clothing and textiles is exciting. There is the thrill that goes with learning how to shop intelligently—the joy of selecting interesting fabrics and seeing smart, wearable garments evolve from them—the fun of learning to use a sewing machine—the feeling of pride and confidence that comes from being well dressed and well groomed. You teachers recognize this, and you work, individually and collectively, not only to heighten that natural drama but to make it more meaningful.

Facts about clothing need to be embroidered with imagination, as well as stitched with practicality.

POSSIBLE ACTS FOR AN INTERPRETIVE STYLE SHOW

One area on which many of you seem to be concentrating is the end-of-the-year style show—figuring how to make it interpret and emphasize what the students have learned, rather than merely show off what they have made.

March of the Fabrics

Idea here is to mount scraps of fabrics (woolen, cotton, and man-made fibers, as acrylic, polyester, nylon, and blends of those fibers with cotton) on both sides of 24×30-inch sheets of cardboard, and then tack them on yardsticks or lengths of lath to make placards that can be carried in the march. Paint the lath, if you like, and outline each mounted scrap with black crayon to suggest that the material has been sewed on with overcast or blanket stitch. Make one or two lettered signs, too.

EDUCATIONAL KITS ARE CHANGING

Are you preparing an educational kit for use in schools? Then by all means, go over your plans with one or more supervisors. Make certain that it not only is acceptable in content, but is in a form that is easy to file and to use.

Commentator introduces act by describing how the year's clothing lessons included a study of fabrics—how to select materials, how to handle them in sewing, etc. As she finishes her brief remarks, six or seven (or any number) of girls enter wearing well-designed outfits, and carrying those placards. They march around the room to lively music, turning their signs first in one direction, then in another, so that everyone in the audience gets a feeling of the wide variety of materials with which the students have been working.

Pin-up Girl and Friend

Commentator begins something like this: "One lesson that was a surprise to most of us was learning to use scissors correctly." She describes this briefly, then goes on to say, "Other lessons had to do with using paper patterns and adjusting them to fit our individual measurements."

After elaborating on this as seems best, she continues: "This act shows Susie Pin-up getting ready to make a skirt and overblouse. Her friend, Jane, has just finished making such an outfit, which she models for you." Girls enter, each wearing tape measure necklaces and carrying giant pairs of cardboard scissors. Susie is wearing a slip, with pieces of pattern pinned in place over it. Jane is dressed in the garments she has made. They promenade to music, twirling their huge scissors as batons, or using them as lorgnettes.

FOR A CLOTHING DISPLAY

Attach a "price tag" to each garment in the display, telling what it cost in the way of materials. Such tags tell quite a story.

Meet the Press

M.C. talks about the importance of pressing in sewing. Shows and describes types of irons used in the course of clothing construction. Relates pressing to the garment or garments about to be modeled.

The Machine Maids

Since many of the grownups in the audience may be interested in what today's sewing machines can do, commentator tells in a few words something about the machines in their sewing room—how many there are, how working time is scheduled so that each girl learns to operate machines and all the attachments. Then the "Machine Maids" appear, some wearing garments that have special ornamental stitching, while others wear or carry aprons decorated with fancy stitches. A smocked dress for a tiny tot is another of many ideas to show the versatility of the modern sewing machine, and the skills the students have acquired.

VELCRO BOARDS

Many teachers are replacing flannel boards with Velcros. Among the firms that can supply materials is the Maharam Fabric Corporation, 1113 So. Los Angeles St., Los Angeles 15, Calif.

Work and Play Parade

Commentator mentions briefly that one of the aims of every clothing course is to encourage students to dress appropriately, with emphasis on the simple life of work and play. Garments modeled might include home dresses, shifts, stretch pants, shell blouses, play shorts—whatever the vogue of the season calls for. One girl might be carrying a new dust mop; another pushing a grocery cart. One might be dressed for a game of tennis; another ready for a picnic—and so on. The more variety, the better.

Through the Looking Glass

After M.C. talks about the attention given to good grooming, well-groomed, well-dressed girls come on the scene. Each carries a huge hand mirror cut from cardboard (painted, of course) with a hole where looking glass would be. As girls promenade, they hold their empty mirror frames to adjust hair or hat, smiling through at the audience as they do so.

These ideas are, of course, merely illustrative of what is being done or might be done in staging interpretive style shows. Possible titles include: "Fun, Fact, and Fashion Show"; "High Show of Styles and Sewing Skills"; "Spring Flower and Fashion Show"—with the acts tying together flower motifs and lessons learned, or similar themes.

SHOE SHOW

For a lesson on footwear, have students bring shoes for showing and discussion. Those half-worn shoes tell a story of misfits and poor postures.

CLOTHING-CENTERED IDEAS FOR BULLETIN BOARDS

These suggestions for bulletin boards and flannel boards, picked up here, there, and everywhere, are mere skeletons of ideas. If any of them appeal, you and your students can bring them to life in your own special way.

Care of Clothing

Cover bulletin board with sky-blue construction paper. At left side mount a big snowman made of fluffy cotton (or white cardboard) with real buttons on his suit and a "stocking cap" cut from red felt. In upper right-hand corner, tip in the opened-up cover of a travel folder that features winter sports. Inside that cover, staple a

BRING ON THE BOYS

Persuade two or three of them to act as escorts in the school style show... Ask one of them to judge a group of pinup pictures showing hairdo's . . . For a P.T.A. meeting, get one of the men teachers to interview a panel of students on "What we have learned in our clothing course."

sheet of paper (same size as folder) on which are typed four or five short, to-the-point rules for taking care of woolen socks, mittens, leather jackets, boots, and the like. In open area of board, use white poster paint to write "Care of Winter Wear."

REMINDERS

Use a string of "come-apart" beads to show how the shape of the face seems to change as the length of the necklace varies . . . Have students model graceful ways to carry gloves, handbag, umbrella, etc. . . . Show interesting ways to wear scarves, stoles, headkerchiefs, etc.

Developing Charm

Cover board with pink or yellow construction paper. At top, paste on a rectangle of black construction paper to suggest an old-time school slate. On it print (with white chalk or paint) "Charm School A.B.C.'s." On the paper below the slate, define the A.B.C.'s, using black crayon for lettering. For example, they might read:

A. "Always Look Interested—and Interesting"
B. "Be Clean Clear Through"
C. "Concentrate on Clothing Care"

Promoting Good Grooming

In one of the top corners of bulletin board pin two hands cut from white paper. On forefinger of one, tie a length of yarn which leads to a white cardboard bowl in opposite corner at bottom of board. Beside the bowl, tip on nail brush and emery board. Caption says: "Remember! Soak; Scrub; Smooth Rough Edges."

THE TOTAL YOU

Students divide into three groups. One works out a head-and-shoulders presentation, showing hair styles, makeup, etc. . . . Second group takes the torso, showing what happens when figure slumps . . . Third works on lower legs and footwear . . . One student is the static model. Screens are arranged so audience sees only what is under discussion. Finally the "total you" emerges.

Creative Decorating

Pockets and Patches. Idea here is to decorate all shapes and sizes of pockets and patches with button designs, fancy stitches, flower cut-outs, or whatever. Scatter them over flannel board or bulletin board.

Button Roundup. String buttons of all kinds on yarn, knotting each in place so that they are well spaced. Swing the string around on bulletin board to suggest a lariat. Put two or three large, very fancy buttons in circle formed, and print caption in some interesting way.

FORESHADOW

Just as the fiction writer builds dramatic impact by foreshadowing what is to come later in the book, so does the teacher build up interest by forecasting what is to happen in the next lesson.

Gift Wraps From Scraps

Decorate and/or tie small boxes and packages with bits of yarn, tape, net, lace, and other trimmings that go with the making of clothing. Thumbtack to board, or hang from push pins. Possibly "write" caption with yarn?

For Easter time, thumbtack a round, straw place mat onto board, for brim of hat. Near center of it, tip on a round box, using double-stick gummed tape. Decorate hat as you like, with flowers, ribbon, etc. In bottom corner of bulletin board tack on a pair of white gloves cut from construction paper. Between hat and gloves write "Happy Easter!"

HAVE YOU TRIED THESE?

- "Import" a ready-made style show from a local store, complete with outside commentator. (Many home economists now are employed by big stores for just such cooperation with schools.)

- Send out complimentary tickets (rather than the usual invitations or announcements) to school style show. This seems to promote greater interest and attendance.

- Borrow a laundry caddy to display garments that, for one reason or another, are not included in show. Since such caddies are on roll-

ONE CLOTHING TEACHER SAYS:

"Since all teen-age girls criticize their mothers, I persuaded a middle-aged friend to pose as a typical mother. Students criticized her hairdo, makeup, walk, clothing, and the like. Snapshots were taken for comparison two weeks later when model returned restyled according to the teens' ideas."

ers they can be wheeled around for all to see. Garments are on hangers, of course.

• At beginning of school year take a candid camera shot of each student. At year's end, take a second shot so that each can observe her own progress in clothes selection and figure improvement.

• Work out an occasional "fun" exhibit for clothing room. One example: A charm necklace to hang on a dress form. (Use plastic lids from coffee cans for the charms. With wax pencil write a grooming reminder on each charm.) Another example: Get boys in shop class to nail a gnarled tree branch to two boards crossed in Christmas-tree-stand fashion. Stand tree on card table. Spray it white if you wish. On it—and on table—display kerchiefs, sun glasses, shorts, pullovers, and other play apparel.

• Extend the clothing idea to make decorative accessories for parties. Some examples: cloth butterflies and flowers pasted on place cards; yarn designs on inexpensive place mats.

• Make a fabric "collage" using bits of cloth instead of tissue paper. Students enjoy letting their imagination go abstract or realistic, according to temperament.

• Braid pieces of material to make frames for oval or round fashion photos, or for hair braids on a class-made mannequin.

These are only a few of many simple original ways you can bring clothing and grooming to life. When you combine this type of class-made creative illustrations with some of the excellent ready-to-use visual aids, you arrive at a new high in student cooperation and enthusiasm. ●

FOR ADDITIONAL IDEAS IN DRAMATIZING CLOTHING SEE CHAPTER 12, ON USING BULLETIN BOARDS.

7.

BUILDING MORE INTEREST IN *Home Planning*

On your job or in volunteer work, are you concerned with helping homemakers make their homes more attractive and livable as well as functional? If you are, you have discovered that while the big subject of home planning, furnishing, and decoration is fascinating to women and girls generally, it is sometimes difficult to dramatize, especially in the classroom.

To bring floor plans, room arrangements, wall finishes, furniture styles, and color harmonies to life, do not lean entirely on photographs and color wheels or other familiar aids. Look around for unusual materials that you can adapt to your purpose. The following illustrative ideas are workable as is. But don't stop with these! Set your creative imagination to work, and you will be surprised at the fresh and original ideas for visuals that will occur to you.

One way to add excitement to home beautification is to use building materials for visuals.

TRY PEG BOARD FOR HOUSE PLANNING

A piece of lightweight peg board (generic name "perforated hardboard") is a ready-made and appropriate aid for demonstrating house planning. The holes measure exactly an inch apart (center to center) which makes it easy to draw on it a plan to scale, allowing one inch to each foot if the board is large enough; otherwise, one inch for each two feet.

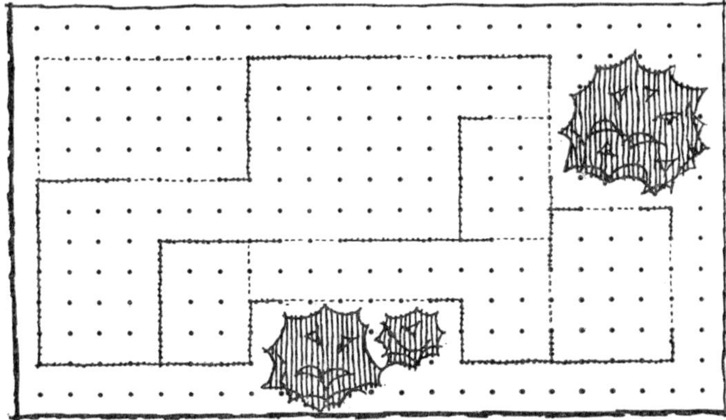

Draw walls with white chalk, indicate doors and windows with dotted lines or with colored chalk. Or, instead of chalk, you might use bright-colored yarns to outline your plan. (Knot end of yarn, pull other end through from underside, stretch to a "break" in your wall; pull yarn down at that point and knot it securely—or jump across the break on underside, as you would in embroidery, then continue the wall.)

If you want to convey something of a 3-dimensional feeling for the house with its surrounding garden, you can fit lengths of uncooked macaroni into the holes for corner posts, and tip on walls of construction paper. Drinking straws can make trunks of trees; bits of old cellulose sponges, dyed green with food coloring or ink, may represent shubbery. The idea, of course, is not to be too realistic or perfect; leave plenty of room for the audience's imagination to work.

ARTISTRY AND HOME DESIGN

We are all born with vision, much of which gets suppressed. The artist is more stubborn than others; he resists the pressure, and the vision remains. That is what makes him an artist. Vision is needed in home decoration, as are imagination, ingenuity, and a feeling for what is good design.

Students will come up with all sorts of ingenious touches.

Where do you get perforated hardboard?

It is sold in lumber yards, in building supply houses, and in some hardware stores and discount houses (a little telephoning will locate it). While it is manufactured in standard 4×8-foot sheets, most dealers will cut it to any desired size. A lightweight grade is often available at bargain rates in 4×4-foot or 2×4-foot pieces—the latter is a good usable size for house plan demonstration.

ABOUT PLASTIC FOAM

If you use this versatile material to any extent, you may like to investigate what florists call a "hot knife"—a saw with an electrically heated wire in place of a blade. With it you can cut plastic foam neatly, can even slice it paper thin. Not expensive. Can be purchased through florist supply houses.

TRY PLASTIC FOAM FOR 3-D DISPLAYS

Squares or other shapes of sparkling white plastic foam, available in the flower-arranging departments of many variety stores at any time of year (and at more modest cost around holiday time) can work wonders in helping to dramatize home-centered information. The crisp, plastic foam is so light and easy to handle and so versatile it suggests any number of uses for itself, once you have a few pieces in hand.

For example, you have a class studying kitchen planning. How can you illustrate the principles of kitchen arrangement to make them more realistic than the usual flat drawings of floor plan and wall elevations?

One possibility: stand three 12-inch squares of inch-thick plastic foam on edge to make three walls for a U-shape kitchen. Overlap corners so that inside measures are 11 inches deep and 12 inches across (i.e., 11×12 feet of floor space). Fasten corners together with toothpicks or thin bamboo skewers or with gummed tape, so they can be taken apart and put together, ad lib.

Since those walls measure 12 inches high, you will probably want to cut off a 3- or 3½-inch strip from top of each square, to bring the ceiling of the kitchen down to a normal 9- or 8½-foot height. Cutting is not difficult. Use a razor blade or sharp knife or a thin-bladed saw.

MODERN SCRAPBOOK

Make an accordion-type display by fastening 8"x 11" cards together with sturdy gummed tape. Mount illustrations of room details on cards. To study, open up file and see the whole display at a glance. Such a portfolio is easy to file.

On the walls, indicate windows and doors, if any, by pinning or taping on shapes cut to scale from construction paper. (You can draw them with crayon, if you wish, but paper cut-outs give greater flexibility.)

After establishing those openings—or before, if you prefer—you are ready to place appliances and cabinets. Those strips left over from the walls can be cut into scalesize refrigerator, range, cupboards, etc., then colored with crayon, to be shifted about to illustrate good and not-so-good work patterns. To show what happens when the refrigerator door opens the wrong way, interrupting the work flow, cut a door from construction paper, fold along one edge to make a hinge, then pin onto the refrigerator so it swings open, first one way, then the other. Much more effective teaching, usually, than merely telling the class to watch out for that problem!

All sorts of innovations are possible, of course, in that tiny model of a kitchen. The use of black-headed pins for drawer pulls; scraps of gingham for curtains; paint or wallpaper represented with colored crayon, and so on and on. How far to go with these doll-house touches would naturally depend on the size and the sophistication of the group.

Backgrounds for display materials are sometimes a problem. Here, too, plastic foam squares are useful, for they attract attention without detracting from the point of the display. Those 12-inch squares are just right for pinning on small samples of related fabrics or color combinations, or photographs, or magazine illustrations, to be passed around from person to person.

In a lecture or demonstration before a large group, a large sheet of plastic foam can be a great help in displaying drapery materials and other fabrics—even samples of carpets. Such sheets are usually available in metropolitan centers, in sizes as large as 2×9 feet. (For information, look in the Yellow Pages of the telephone directory under "Plastics—Foam." The first firm you call may not handle the type you want, but will usually refer you to a source.) If large sheets are not to be had, you can fit smaller pieces together to make the size you want, and glue them with white glue (such as Elmer's). Some other types of glue contain a solvent that breaks down the plastic foam.

PROPORTION

A brief study of modern low-ceilinged rooms is eye opening. One sees the appropriateness of the low-slung furniture in use today.

TURN A BIG, STURDY CARTON INTO A PORTABLE EXHIBIT

You have a double problem: (1) you want to show swatches of curtain materials, upholstery fabrics, carpet samples, illustrations of types of furniture, against various popular wall finishes; and (2) you will have to transport your own display, so it must not be too elaborate or awkward to handle.

Answer: Find a big, deep, sturdy corrugated-paper carton, preferably with a square, or almost square, bottom. Finish each of its four walls on the *outside* in a different way: one painted a light color, one painted a deeper tone, one covered with wallpaper and one with a thin sheet of stained plywood, glued in place. These illustrate four of the most common types of walls found in homes.

Pack those fabrics and other display materials in the box, ready to go.

At the meeting, after unpacking and arranging those materials in order of presentation, set

MODELS

Home economists who work in redevelopment areas frequently find it difficult to interest displaced families in their new homes. Miniature models showing good room arrangements seem to be one of the best devices.

the empty box on a table, placed so that the audience sees only one wall at a time, while you discuss its advantages and disadvantages and show its harmony or lack of harmony with certain types of fabrics and furnishing. For the most dramatic contrast, start with the dark wood paneling; drape against it a thin, white curtain material, then compare this effect with a colorful, patterned, heavier drapery. Now turn the box and show the white curtain against the wallpapered background. You can go whatever direction you like. One thing sure, you will have active and vocal audience participation in that kind of teaching show.

USE PAINT CHIPS TO TEACH COLOR HARMONY

An assortment of those little painted paper samples which every paint dealer has on display can be of as much help in studying color combinations in class as they are in deciding what tint or shade of a color to paint one's home kitchen or a piece of furniture. The visuals that follow illustrate two of many possible ways to use them.

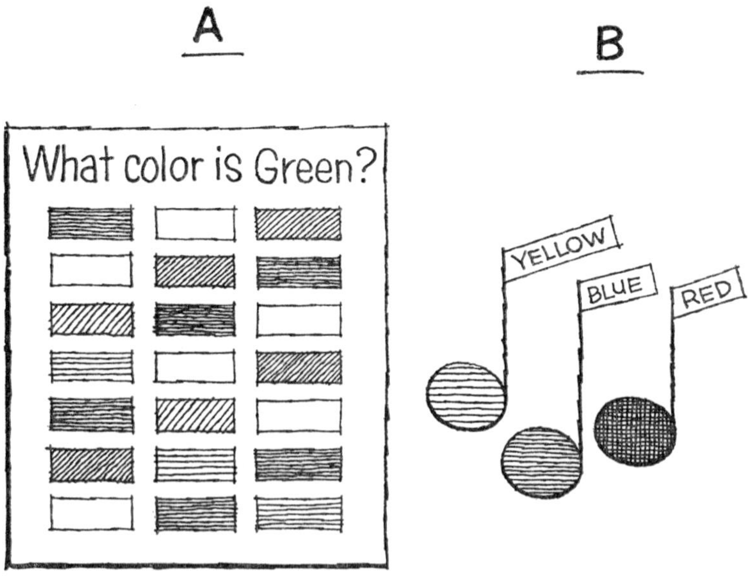

Visual A. Many paint manufacturers group varying shades of each color in little panels so that one can see at a glance the range of tones that are available in a certain brand of paint. Mount these as suggested, then discuss which shades of green (for example) would seem most appropriate for floor covering; which ones would perhaps be best for a painted coffee table; which ones for walls, and for which types of rooms. (A breakfast room with apple green walls and sparkling white furniture could be most interesting, whereas a narrow hall painted dark green might be repelling.)

INSTANT DRAMATIZATION

One extension specialist uses the chalk board to teach proportion in furniture. Vertical lines of various lengths represent tall pieces of furniture, as cabinets, room dividers, or floor-to-ceiling lamps. Horizontal lines stand for sofas, tables, chairs, and the like.

Visual B. Cut paint chips into ovals to suggest musical notes, then group them in three's to show good combinations. Example: (1) dark blue floor; (2) yellow walls; (3) accents of red.

COMPARE CURTAINS TO CLOTHING

For a visual lesson with actual samples or pictures, how about likening window-wear to girls' and women's dresses? Start the session by asking, "Do windows look better in short dresses, long dresses, or 2-piece outfits (i.e., cafe curtains)?" This gives an opportunity to discuss sill lengths and floor lengths, and to discourage that awkward in-between length. Curtains for a dinette, for example, usually come just to the sill; in a more formal dining room, floor length curtains might be preferable.

Curtains for kitchens, like house dresses, are short, crisp, trim, and washable. Bedroom draperies should be restful—perhaps a bit frilly for daughter's room though not for the master bedroom. Draperies for formal rooms (like a girl's formals) can be either slim-line or full and flowing.

SHAPES

Decorators (more properly called "interior designers") now encourage their clients to understand the need for some variation in furniture shapes. A round table, for example, breaks up the monotony of rectangles and squares.

Large windows (like large girls) should wear curtains that do not look skimpy or thick and heavy. An over-tall window (like an over-tall girl) may need to have its height minimized—perhaps with a valance board, or with cafe curtains. Commenting that there are fashions in window-wear just as there are fashions in clothing leads naturally into displaying new curtain and drapery materials, and newer types of window shades.

However you put it together and whatever points you stress, this has the makings of an interesting lesson, especially when you work in such practical information as how to shorten or lengthen curtains; how to handle drip-dry materials; the importance of preshrinking, and the like.

HOUSE TOUR

One way to make sure that your group tour of houses will prove truly educational and effective is to give advance assignments. As an example, one homemaker could make special notes of color schemes, another of window treatments, etc. At a follow-up meeting, reports are given and discussed.

FUN PROJECT

In one group of do-it-yourself decorators, each homemaker brought in a "home beautification" item costing less than 50 cents, and told how it might be used. The ingenuity displayed was inspiring.

CARPET DISPLAY

One home advisor prevailed upon a carpet manufacturer to give her a quantity of samples. Mounted they made an interesting display for the study of colors and textures in relation to room color schemes.

FURNITURE BUYMANSHIP

Subject of this lesson might be, "Try out this sofa (or other piece of furniture) in your own living room." Begin by showing picture of sofa. If feasible, project it on a screen so that all may study it. Describe its color; length; type of material; kind of wood; price range. In other words, bring it to life. Then start discussion with such questions as: Would this be sensible in a home where there are small children? Would it fit into rooms of various sizes, in case the family moves? For that reason, would a 2-sectioned sofa be more practical—or what disadvantages might it have? Could the sofa be made into a comfortable emergency bed? Will the fabric hold up, be easily cleaned? At what price do you consider it a good buy? Many more will be offered.

Final discussion brings up the personal question: Would you buy this sofa for your present home, or the home you hope to have? If so, why? If no, why not? Object here is, of course, to relate all decorating to the needs and tastes of the family.

THOUGHTS TO WORK INTO DISCUSSIONS

- The importance of using art objects importantly—not tentatively.

- The need for a "touch of lipstick" in most rooms—perhaps a cushion in a just-right shade of red; a small, tight arrangement of red carnations or other flowers; a red cigarette box; or a big, red candle.

- The problem of a roomful of legs! In Grandmother's day when women's skirts were longer than they are now, the legs of most pieces of furniture were sturdier and more decorative. Also they were partially hidden by those long skirts, therefore were less obvious. Discuss ways of concealing or playing down at least a few of those thin, straight legs on today's chairs, sofas, tables, and cabinets, such as using a floor-length slipcover on one or two chairs in a room—hanging a cabinet on the wall instead of standing it on legs—covering a round table with a floor-length felt topper.

- The danger of too many little things in a room at one time. Emphasize, perhaps show, well-designed small items, as good pottery bowls, candlesticks, ash trays, or pillows, then gently discourage an overprofusion of knick-knacks.

Every woman finds basic principles in home planning, furnishing, and otherwise beautifying are easy to learn by rote. But when she is faced with making choices of color, pattern, texture,

MORE PICTORIALS—LESS TALK

The old way of teaching decorating was to use wordy descriptions. Modern way is to do it with pictures. In other words, "Pictorialize; don't editorialize."

LESSON FROM A HOUSE PLANT

One decorator says, "A $10 plant often does more for a room than a $40 piece of furniture." Discuss how to display a plant to best advantage. One idea: Set the pot in a paper bucket such as painters use. The design is good; the white effective; the cost negligible.

design of a piece of furniture or a set of window draperies for her own home, she is bewildered.

That is why the dynamic use of visuals is so important in this area. Seeing is not enough. Discussion—live discussion—is needed in order to relate rules to reality. Only in that way can one promote greater awareness and the development of surer judgment in one's students, whether young or older. ●

CHAPTERETTE: *Paper-and-Pencil Visuals*

WHAT YOU WRITE on the chalk board will ordinarily be copied into individual notebooks. But to what extent have you explored the possibilities of paper-and-pencil visuals beyond the natural hookup with the chalk board?

For one illustration: You are talking to a group of students or homemakers about the elements that go into making a living room livable. At the onset you suggest that each draw a large rectangle on one page of her notebook to represent a living room. This gives you an opportunity to discuss room proportions, and enables those in the audience to visualize their imaginary rooms.

Big advantage of paper-and-pencil visuals is that they encourage audience participation—which is one of the top secrets of showmanship.

Next you outline the elements that go into planning such a room. To provide a memory key, talk about the *Seven C's*—Comfort; Convenience; Circulation (i.e., keeping walk-through areas open); Color harmony; Charm; Cost (both original and upkeep); and Conversation. This last C should be considered from two aspects. First, there should be groupings of chairs and sofas to make it easy to converse. And second, there should be a few "conversation pieces" in every room: perhaps a family heirloom, an interesting personal collection—anything that invites comment and conversation.

Learn to edit your own copy ruthlessly. If you do not do this, someone else very likely will!

One thing is certain: Any time you can tie paper-and-pencil activity into a presentation, you double attention value. ●

8.

Family Relations

ARE EASILY DRAMATIZED

DOES your work load include the teaching of Family Relations, or interpreting some phase of it to a nonschool group? If so, you have developed a series of lesson plans, or an approach, that fits your particular audience. You know where to go for suitable filmstrips and pertinent information. You are aware of the most recent recommendations as to what should be stressed and why and how. But you may still be looking for auxiliary devices that will help to bring your sessions to life. If that is the case, see what you can do with these visuals:

Good family relationships are made up of little things. So are meaningful lessons on the subject.

CHALK BOARD GRAPHICS

(Skeletons of ideas to be clothed in your own words)

In the diagram immediately following, Figure *A* illustrates how difficult it is to draw a freehand circle. Figure *B* shows how simple it is to do so when you use two pieces of chalk on the ends of a short length of string.

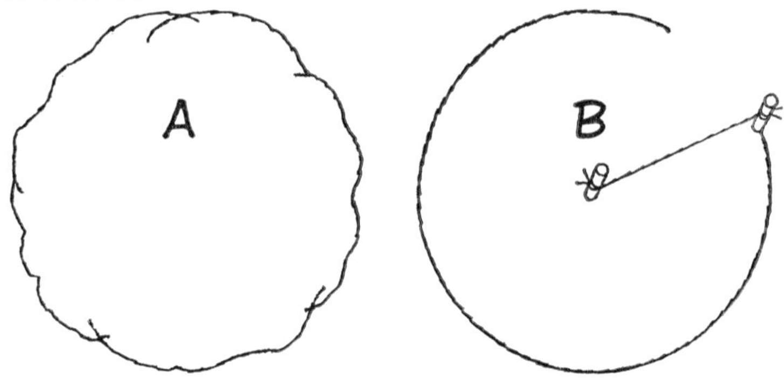

Interpretation of Visual. Every person—particularly the young person—is trying to make a well-rounded world for himself or family. With nothing to tie to (that is without cooperation) it is like trying to draw that freehand circle. The young person with a well-adjusted family around him is fortunate, because there is someone to help him round out his world. But the boy or girl who has no one on "the other end of the string" needs to seek help from a teacher, counselor, or community advisor, and the assistance is always there if it is wanted. Just as the size of the circle depends upon the length of the string, one's world depends upon the extent of his ambitions. Just as the two pieces of chalk must work together, parents must do the same—not pull in opposite directions.

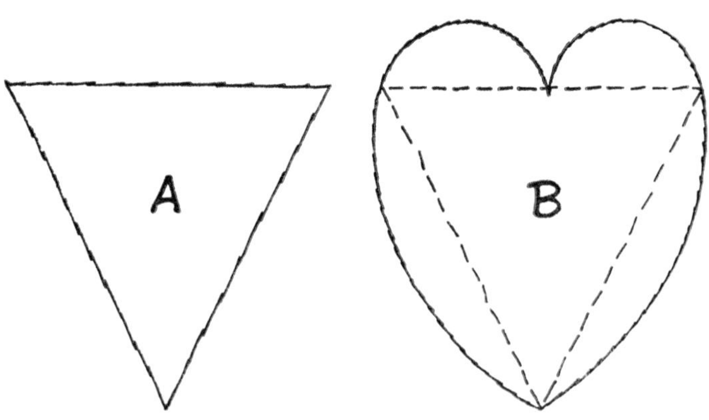

Interpretation of Visual. Triangle *A* represents a family in which one or more members are rigid, uncompromising, uncooperative. When this is the case, a triangle exists—perhaps it has to do with a disagreement over money, or a division of work, or a difference of opinion on almost anything. In a home dominated by personal rigidity, there is little warmth and understanding. But Figure *B* illustrates how easy it is to turn that hard, triangle symbol into a figure that represents a gentle-heart approach. All it takes is a little bending on the part of everyone concerned.

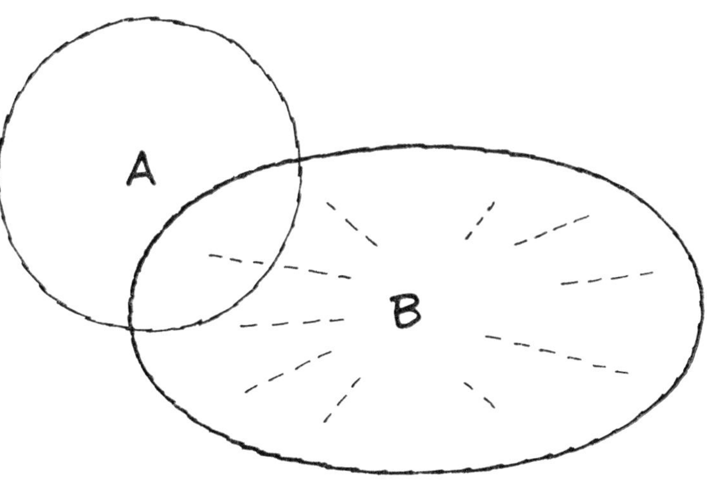

Interpretation of Visual. The old-time concept of the family circle is represented in *A* as in pioneer times when all life revolved around the family as a close-knit unit. (Recreation consisted of reading aloud, singing, games such as checkers and dominoes which everyone in the family watched and advised while the others played, and so on.) *B* is today's picture, indicating that family interests have broadened, become more a part of the life of the community. Discussion brings out arguments for and against young persons'

stretching the boundaries of the family circle to build lives of their own—to go into orbit, as the figure suggests.

According to one survey, advertising based upon knowledge and skills had a 7% return; based on attitudes and emotions, 93%. Family living is the emotional side of home economics—returns from it are great.

PRELUDES TO CLASS DISCUSSIONS

Has it been your experience that once a lesson or a presentation is under way it gathers momentum and interest, but that the problem is how to get it off the ground? Ideas such as the ones that follow not only serve as launching pads for discussion, but suggest small lessons in themselves.

- Before you state a problem or ask a question, announce that no one is to speak out until a 30-second think period has been observed. Idea is to encourage students to think before they advance an opinion—a good habit to adopt when participating in family discussions with which everyone is at times involved.

- Discourage students from prefacing all their remarks with those odious words, "I think." Remind them of this at the beginning of the discussion. Try to get them to use phrases such as "It seems to me," or "As I see it," or "Perhaps this is a thought." In family arguments those words "I think" are often fighting words. A little discipline along this line will not only help students to proceed more objectively, but it may even help to eliminate some of the tiresome "I thinks" so prevalent in speeches, discussions, and conversations.

QUESTION

Is "family living" a more definitive term than homemaking to describe home economics at the secondary level? Might not the policymakers be more receptive to it? Surely "family living" includes all phases of homemaking—food, clothing, shelter, personal relationships, money management, etc.

- Combine a lesson in family living with one designed to promote social graces. For example, three members of the class are chosen: one to represent the mother, another her daughter, and the third, the girl's friend. Girl's assignment is to introduce her friend to her mother, after which class comments, questions, or criticizes. You then suggest the need to make introductions more interpretive, as "Mother, this is Sue Carter. She is in our Foods IV Group." Then, aside to Sue, "Mother works part time as a nurse at Children's Hospital." Idea here, of course, is to encourage students to communicate more fully and gracefully, as well as to show pride in one's family and friends. Such an activity takes only a few minutes at the beginning of the lesson, and is frequently worth much.

• In a session that emphasizes the need to understand one's ancestry, bring in a large map of the United States, mounted on cork board. For roll call, ask each student to mention the home state or country of a parent or grandparent. Monitor sticks pins into the map accordingly. If ancestors come from another country, pins go outside boundaries of ours. Make an occasional comment, as "Texas is the second largest state, exceeded only by Alaska." And so on. Pride in family and in country is often developed in ways such as this.

OLD SAYING

"When does a boy become a man? When there is a need for him to do so." **Lessons in family living are really lessons in growing up—in learning to think and behave as responsible adults.**

A STUDY IN WORDS

For a group of students who pride themselves on their sophistication, it is a good idea to discuss the true meanings of some of the words used so freely in conversations that have to do with problems in living. For example:

Understand. The word literally means "stand under." When a youth complains that his parents or teachers do not understand him, he is really saying he wants them to stand under him—to keep him from falling.

Insecurity. To make a house secure means to lock it against danger. To secure a boat is to tie it to the dock. When one complains about feeling insecure, is he saying he really wants to be tied down, locked in from the world, made safe from life?

Reject. Literally, this means to refuse. But before anything can be refused, it must be offered. The person who feels rejected may well ask himself whether or not he has offered anything in the way of cooperation with his family or with society.

Frustration. Although the dictionary would not countenance such a definition, isn't frustration really "first-ration"—wanting to be first in everything? And isn't that desire to be first the usual cause of the frustrated person's problem?

Underprivileged. According to the dictionary, "privilege" is a right enjoyed beyond the common advantage of others. When one says he is "under"-privileged, he is not asking for a fair and equal chance; he is saying he feels sorry for himself because he is not among the privileged few.

Seeing such words in a new light may prove to be eye-openers that will be remembered for a long time to come.

TV AGAIN

Do so-called "soap operas" affect the lives of students? Who knows? Certainly they remind the listener that life is not all sweetness and light for anyone—which is a lesson that must somehow be learned. As screenwriters say, "Any family's private life would make a television serial!"

BABY IN CLASS

One home economics teacher asked a friend to bring her year-old baby to a class in family relations. As baby played in his playpen, mother talked informally of how a baby changes the family living pattern. Students asked questions. Session had reality.

A BROADENED VIEW OF FAMILY RELATIONSHIPS

Along with exploring the true meanings of words, a look at the term Family Relationships itself is in order. That is, the word "family" can, and does, mean more than a group living under one roof—it suggests the great human family. The word "relations" has to do with all things in relation to all other things and all other people. Students need to be reminded frequently that their thinking and actions must be in relation to the welfare of others (whether of the family or of the world) as against selfcenteredness.

And why not a new theory of "Family Relativity," complete with formula! Professor Einstein might not approve the following, but perhaps it will inspire you to improve upon it:

$$G.F.R. = U^2 \times P^n$$

Translated, it means Good Family Relations equals Understanding, squared, times Patience, raised to the nth power! ●

SITUATIONS REPORT

Family life drama is hidden in the columns of every newspaper. Perhaps students need to be urged to try to read between the lines.

AMATEUR PSYCHOANALYSIS

Many teen-agers have become more concerned with behavior patterns by "analyzing" the tendencies they observe in younger brothers and sisters. By trying to understand others, they learn to understand themselves.

9.

NEW DIMENSIONS FOR *Home Equipment* PRESENTATIONS

Utility dramatizations, like utilities themselves, have resources that have never been tapped. Explore them.

MOST PRESENTATIONS that center around home equipment and appliances have a distinct personality—a come-alive style all their own. Why? The answers are obvious.

First of all, you who are concerned with homemaking conveniences are working constantly with things that are sparkling new. Those late-model ranges, new-style washers, multipurpose cleaners and the like give you something fresh to talk about or write about. They fill you with an enthusiasm that is automatically transferred to your audience. As a result, your material has a march-along tempo.

Second, you are in close touch with actual homemakers. They bring their questions and problems to your home service centers. They learn to know you — and you learn to know them—through your home calls, demonstrations, and dramatizations. You meet many of them personally when you show your slides or filmstrips to club groups. And all such contact is the feedback that helps you to put reality into your presentations—a reality which invariably heightens dramatic appeal.

Third, through your newsletters (such as The Distaffer and Home Service Exchange) you are kept up to date with what others in your field are doing. This free exchange of ideas stimulates your own thinking, challenges you to outthink and outdo your friendly competitors!

All these factors added together help you to sell your ideas and information to today's and tomorrow's homemakers. Question is, *what can you sell besides convenience, and the pride that goes with having a well-equipped home?*

MENTAL POWER PLANT

Every home economist concerned with equipment needs to build a power plant in her own mind in order to generate imagination and ideas.

THE BROADENED VIEW

This is one way to reason: More and more homemakers, freed from some of their household tasks by modern equipment, are able to devote time and energy to community problems. Why not occasionally remind them that home appliances and aids actually contribute to the welfare of the entire community, rather than just to their individual owners? How good lighting, for example, inside and outside, makes for greater safety; serves as a deterrent for crime. How modern laundry equipment and automated cleaning devices make for more sanitary homes, thus promoting better health for the community. How smoke-free heating and cooking equipment help to solve the smog problem.

And, farfetched though it may sound, how these exciting modern appliances and devices can even be useful in warding off juvenile delinquency where it usually has its beginnings—in the family. As everyone knows, that sad problem can and does develop in many a "comfortable" home. Your audience would, of course, question such a thought that household equipment could possibly help a boy or girl develop into a responsible young citizen. But it can.

THE TAPE RECORDER

Do you make a tape recording of interviews as you help homemakers solve individual problems? Later playbacks will give you fresh lines to use in your presentations; may show you where and how to improve your interviewing techniques.

To begin with, every youngster demands activity; and the more important and "grown up" the activity is, the more satisfying it is. Little children are excited about learning, doing, helping. True, their "help" may be questionable, but if it is encouraged, responsibility develops fast. The point is, old-time "chores" were pretty dull and depressing, but operating today's mechanical devices is exciting. And when excitement can follow a constructive route, there is less inclination on the part of most youngsters to seek the destructive.

DRAMA

One of the most effective devices used in dramatizing information is to quote what some other homemaker has done to solve similar problems.

Perhaps there are ways to point out some of these far-reaching facts to the leaders of club groups who are always looking for new approaches to today's problems. Just as they are always looking for qualified speakers who have something to say in depth!

WHAT'S NEW

Food pages in many newspapers feature a "What's New in Foods" column. Perhaps some of these might be expanded to point up more frequently what's new in equipment and appliances. You would, of course, need to telescope important features into a sentence or two. You could not be wordy.

TAKE ADVANTAGE OF HOBBIES, TOO

As you are well aware, many homemakers, along with being interested in their homes and families and community, spend many hours with their hobbies such as playing bridge, collecting antiques, going on house tours, or studying art. Is there something more that you might do to capitalize on those activities—especially in the mature-aged group which usually has the money to update their home equipment?

Kitchen Antique Show

For example, have you ever staged a Kitchen Antique Show against a background of up-to-the-minute kitchen equipment (as in a home service center)? Some of the ideas that might be carried out effectively include a peg board of old-time egg beaters and hand whisks to be hung above a new-model electric beater or blender. A display of sadirons on an old-style ironing board, with a shining steam iron importantly posed on a new-type board nearby. Pictures or stylized art of early-day cook stoves and wood-and-coal ranges mounted on a poster to hang above a brand-new range. An 1890 cookbook beside a new one right off the presses. Even Grandmother's kitchen rocking chair alongside a modern kitchen stool.

The possibilities are many—and many a collector and admirer of antiques has been known to stop and study the new appliances, even though her hobby is centered in the past.

HAVE YOU EVER

Used 5 or 6 green or blue safety night lights in a room to create an eerie setting for a home Hallowe'en party? They are safer than candles . . . And have you ever suggested (in a leaflet or demonstration) that those low-power night lights make acceptable low-cost gifts?

Art and Flower Shows

And have you ever turned over your testing kitchens to a Kitchen Art Show planned by a small group of local artists or art students? In the modern home with its many windows and built-ins, space for pictures is limited. As a result, many artists with a flair for design and color are doing what they speak of as "kitchen poster art" (featuring vegetables, fruits, interesting cooking pots, and the like) for use inside cabinet doors, corners in dinettes, walls in family rooms and even the house walls of patios. Such a display with a brief talk by one of the artists should bring a special group of homemakers to your home service center. And what they see there will be more than art work. They will see, also, your new refrigerators and ranges and dish-washers.

And have you set up a Service Center Flower Show, with several outstanding Japanese arrangements displayed on range, refrigerator, cabinets, and the like, to create an exciting atmosphere that leads into a film (or slides) of Oriental food

FOOD MODELS

Static displays of kitchen equipment benefit by introducing food into the setup. Since actual foods lose their freshness, wax models are a good answer. One firm that can supply them is Imitation Food Display Company, 107 Lawrence St., Brooklyn 1, N.Y.

By the way, your state extension service undoubtedly keeps an up-to-date file as to where all types of visual materials can be purchased.

specialties? Or added a style show of aprons from all over the world to dramatize a film showing of "Foods From Many Lands?"

Indirect approaches such as these can, and often do, lead to direct sales. Which is, of course, one of the things for which you are working.

MORE IDEAS

To capitalize on the present-day interest in house tours, would there be anything in inviting a small group (as a specific study club) to a progressive home appliance tour in a large department store? First stop in the "tour" might be the lamp department where a home economist talks about home lighting, showing what happens when a light globe of one size or tone is replaced with one of greater—or less—wattage. She will have many more ideas to present.

After a few minutes spent on lamps and lighting, the group moves on to the department (or part of the store) where washers and driers are on display. Here the activity might center around a practical demonstration of how to launder some of the newer fabrics. Since it is not likely that the machines can be actually put into operation, the demonstration will probably need to be a static one in which are shown garments that have been improperly—and properly—laundered.

The next move could be on into the small appliance department of the store for a question-and-answer forum, followed by simple, prepared-in-advance refreshments, and a few minutes of friendly chitchat. Result: the club group has spent a pleasant afternoon learning about new appliances, and you have met those homemakers on a personal basis. ●

POSSIBLE WINDOW DISPLAY

If your home service center has window space available, you may wish to consider this idea: Move out or close off all equipment. Hang one or more works of art against a good background. Show ways of lighting or spotlighting the paintings. In same display call attention to a leaflet on the subject.

10.

Money Management

MADE MEANINGFUL WITH VISUALS

A collection of usable ideas that add up to compounded interest in planned spending and saving.

WHEN YOU SHOW a group of students how to cut and sew a pretty blouse or make and serve a puffy omelet, the lessons come through because you are working with tangibles. From then on a student can, by referring to her memory or her notes, make blouses and/or omelets. But when you talk about buymanship and home finances, you are dealing with variables, and what seem to be intangibles. Concrete visuals and visual expressions are definitely needed to bring such subject matter to life, make it more meaningful and applicable to each individual. The visual-making ideas that follow have worked for others, and can be made workable for you.

A NEW LOOK AT THE DOLLAR

In all courses that have to do with personal or family finance, one basic aim is to teach an awareness of values. And one way to get a series of such lessons off to a good start is to take a few minutes to analyze the dollar sign itself.

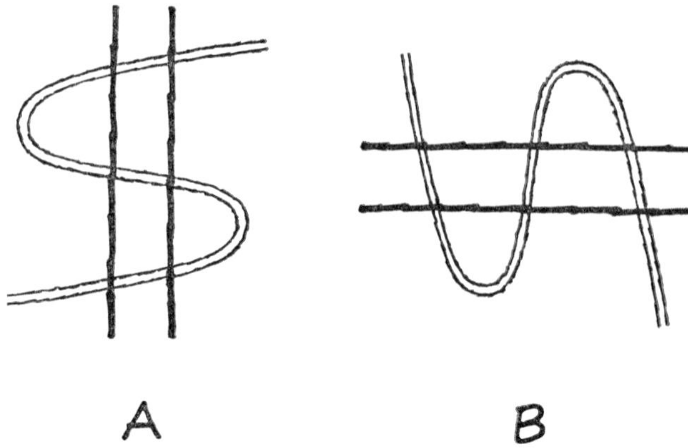

A B

Begin by making a dollar sign on the chalk board or on cardboard, then explain what it represents. For present purposes, the two parallel straight lines stand for income and outgo. Continuing the analysis, see how the dollar sign looks lying down. Here the curved line shows the normal ups and downs of any budget. Important thing is to keep income and outgo as nearly in line as possible, even though there may be temporary fluctuations.

INTRODUCTION TO BUDGET MAKING

The visual on opposite page is designed to show future homemakers how to work out a budget. Begin lesson by having members of the class suggest all of the items that must come out of the family pay check. Write them under *A*. Next show how to put those items into four basic boxes, as shown by *B*. Next discuss what a family's monthly income might be. Figure indicated here is $400, but any figure can be used.

First deduct a reasonable amount for shelter, Box 1. Visual indicates $100 a month—which opens up a discussion of what a family would likely need to spend for rent in their locality.

Next comes Box 2—food. How many dollars of the $400 must be allowed for this? Is $100 about right? (This discussion will be exciting!) At this point the young homemaker begins to see

MONEY MANAGEMENT FOR LOW-INCOME FAMILIES

Your professional publications do a fine job of reporting on this subject. It is good to read such quotes as, "Our women call their group a club, not a class. They meet to 'talk things over,' not to be talked to, or told what to do."

how much of that pay check must go for just two things—shelter and food. Now she sees that those installment payments, included in Box 3, will need to be kept to a minimum if she has much of anything left for all of those expenses that must come out of Box 4—which includes clothing, medical costs, haircuts, cosmetics, recreation, gifts, and all such incidentals.

All of this is, of course, a rough idea to be ironed out to fit the specific group. Object is to get young people to understand something of the problem of living within a certain income.

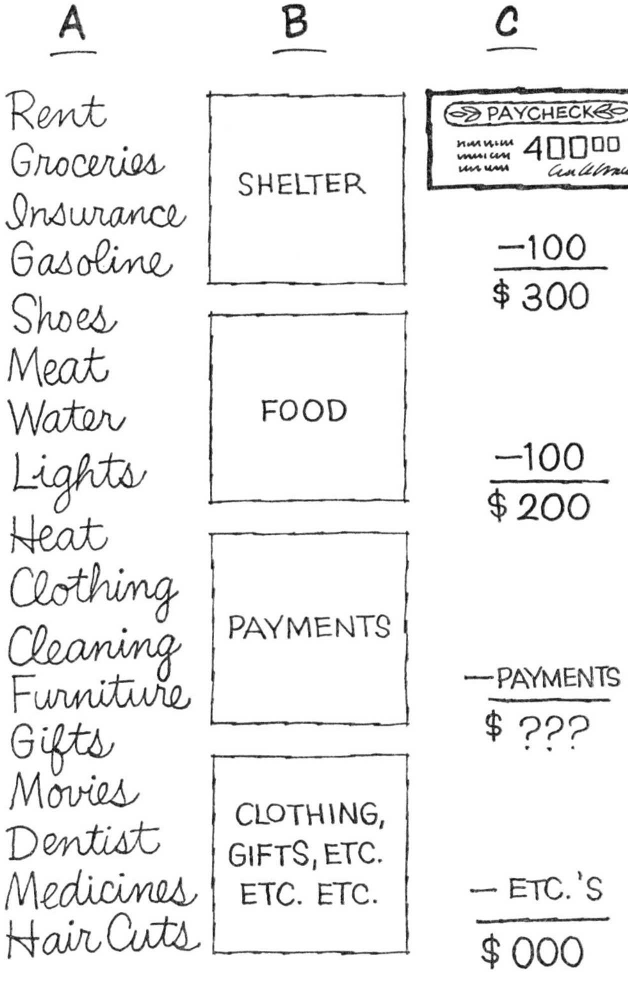

A

Rent
Groceries
Insurance
Gasoline
Shoes
Meat
Water
Lights
Heat
Clothing
Cleaning
Furniture
Gifts
Movies
Dentist
Medicines
Hair Cuts

B

SHELTER

FOOD

PAYMENTS

CLOTHING, GIFTS, ETC. ETC. ETC.

C

PAYCHECK 400.00

−100
$ 300

−100
$ 200

—PAYMENTS
$???

— ETC.'S
$ 000

LUXURY CALENDAR

Encourage students and homemakers to keep a private calendar in which they jot down those extra expenses. As, "Jan's wedding gift cost $8.75, plus $1 for wrappings." "We spent $26.30 on our trip to the city." Such a notation of where the money really went is eye opening!

TWO MONEY-MANAGEMENT VISUALS THAT APPEAL TO YOUNG PEOPLE

All young people realize that skill in the various sports comes about through hard work and discipline. Visuals such as these, relating to sports and recreation, offer many openings for classroom conversations.

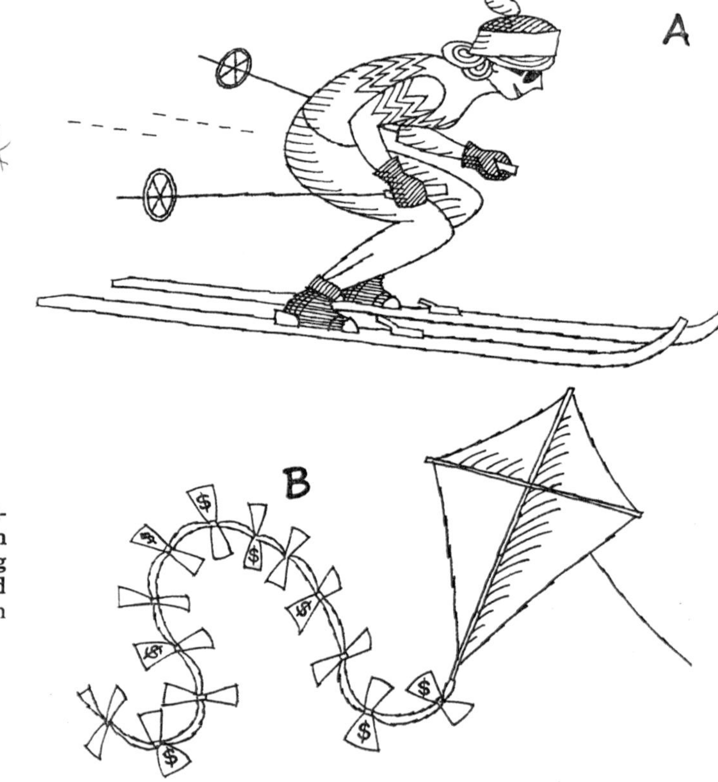

Strength in communications depends largely on judgment. In knowing what is right to say and how to say it—and when and where!

Interpretation of Visual. The figure on skis, using ski poles, in Visual *A*, brings out this thought: Just as the skier needs strength, skill, and discipline to tackle the long slope, the young homemaker can take surer strides toward good money management when she is equipped with good health, homemaking skills, and the balance and discipline that help her to keep her budget in line. Discussion brings out the financial value of good health, which can be built up in one's early years with the help of good nutrition, and the added value of such skills as sewing, cooking, and the like, which also can be developed early in life. Comment emphasizes the ski poles—the balance needed to keep one's feet on sound financial ground.

One homemaker said, *"I want to be treated as an average homemaker, not as an underprivileged mother on a low income."*

The tail of a kite as shown in Visual *B* illustrates the need to allow for recreation in planning a family budget. Just as every kite needs a useless-looking tail to balance it in the wind, every family needs a little fun to keep it balanced in the face of difficulties and problems. When, however, you study the tail of a kite, you will see that it is usually made up of little bits of paper and cloth that would otherwise be wasted. In like manner, family recreation must usually come out of small economies here and there. Each of these economies in itself is insignificant, but when all are strung together they can produce something spectacular.

Going on from there, you might suggest that the four sides of the kite frame represent the four major divisions of a family budget. For a clincher to the lesson, point out that not only must the kite have balance, but that someone must hold tight to the string (i.e., the family money plan) that keeps kite, tail and all, afloat.

SIDE EFFECTS

Insist that students keep all records neatly. Who knows? Many of them may eventually find jobs in banks and in other places of business where neatness as well as accuracy is important.

MORE ABOUT SMALL ECONOMIES

The tail of the kite is, of course, only one way to dramatize how small savings can add up to good times or to savings accounts which, in turn, provide for future comfort and enjoyment. Have you tried either of these activities to stress this point?

Mythical Savings Account

Suggest that individual students write down, for one week, every nonessential purchased, together with the price. List might include excess buying of such things as soft drinks that have no appreciable food value (suggest reading of labels); impulse buying of clothing that is not needed, and so on. At end of the week each student adds up how much might have been saved had she not spent money needlessly. If you doubt that individuals will keep such records, introduce the idea in a class discussion.

POSTER IDEA

In dominant spot, draw or mount a big bird cage, with door open. Birds of all colors are flying out, each "bird" representing a type of expense. Tag line reads: *"You can't recapture these birds once they get away."*

Wastebasket Suggests Waste

For another visual, fill a small wastebasket with crumpled pieces of paper on which have been written examples of waste. During a lesson on small economies, empty wastebasket onto table and read some of the notes—as keeping electric heaters or blankets or lights turned on when they are not needed; carelessness in turning off water tap tightly; using more detergent than is needed or recommended; wasting foil, waxed paper, and the like; buying and cooking more vegetables than will be eaten; spoiling food by burning; or ruining clothing by careless laundering, and so on.

CHALLENGE

Along with teaching money management, put yourself to the test. Examples: Figure out how a homemaker can stretch $2 to produce a satisfying dinner for four . . . What part of a recommended clothing allowance probably goes for shoes alone . . . How a girl can make her own clothes if she has no sewing machine . . . These are problems that homemakers face. If you do not understand them, how can you solve them?

LESSONS IN CONSUMER BUYING

A great deal of your money-wise teaching does, of course, center around Consumer Education. Since, however, much of what is stressed today may (it is hoped!) be legally corrected tomorrow, most of the emphasis might well be put on Consumer Understanding. Everyone needs understanding and realization of what one has to spend; what are necessities and what are comparative trifles; what are best buys; what purchases contain hidden costs—as extra interest rates in certain buying plans. Additional understanding is needed of the problems related to the things one buys—the problems of growers, packers, business firms, and all others concerned with industry.

The homemaker may, for example, say to herself or in class that 39 cents a pound for asparagus is exorbitant. But when discussion brings out some of the problems of the asparagus farmer --that he has but one crop a year; that the land on which asparagus is grown is high priced and taxes are heavy; that labor costs run high—then that price-per-pound has a different meaning:

If a homemaker or student shows concern over how little her food dollars buy, you may need to suggest that not all purchases in a market are food—try grouping actual foods at one end of the cart, and nonfood items at the other end, and have the two groups rung up separately. This invariably is a step toward consumer understanding.

If someone remarks that prices in restaurants, bakeshops, and the like are out of line with what food supplies cost in the market, analyze the problem. Foodstuffs are just one part of the restaurant owner's costs of doing business, just as wheat is only one part of the baker's costs of making a loaf of bread. Also to be considered are rent; liability insurance; expensive equipment; license fees; upkeep (cleaning, repairs, redecorating, etc.); breakage; salaries and wages of cooks, bakers, clerks, waitresses, janitors, and other help; plus the losses that occur when food goes unsold

FACE FACTS

Show how to make a simple financial map of the year ahead, using a manila file folder. Open it up; divide space into 12 sections, heading them Jan., Feb., etc. In each box list all "must-pay" items that fall due that month — insurance payments, all kinds; taxes, all kinds; dues, assessments, etc. Use that same folder to hold bills payable for the current month.

INCENTIVE

The artist is oblivious to his basic needs because he has a dream. Can more be done to put practicality into the dreams and ambitions of those who have financial worries?

and cannot be offered for sale the next day. All of these—and more—throw a realistic light on those costs.

AGE-OLD DEVICE

Try to get homemakers (especially those on limited incomes) to talk about what they hope for their chidren. When they can do that, they are open to suggestions as to how to manage.

LINES THAT LEAD TO OPEN COMMUNICATIONS

Serve Your Budget Sunny-side Up. Help students and homemakers to see that money managing is not a negative, restricting thing, but a positive step toward actually living better on one's income whatever it may be.

The High Cost of Free Time. Comment on how to plan activities that make for interesting recreation without overspending. A picnic field trip to find beautiful pebbles for making mosaics, for one example.

The "NO How" of Money Managing. That is, the strength to say "no" to extravagances.

A Look at the IF in Gift Giving. If, for example, one mother in a community said "No presents" on the invitations to her child's birthday party, other mothers would do the same—and leaks in a dozen budgets would be promptly stopped!

GRIN vs. GRIM

Budgets are serious matters, but they need not be grim. Writing on that subject years ago, Ellis Parker Butler said, "If you have only a baby blanket to keep you warm, there is no point in cutting it up into little pieces and spreading it around over your body. What you need is a bigger blanket!" Quoting such a statement may put a brighter complexion on the serious facts at hand.

WHEN YOU WRITE ABOUT MONEY

As you have doubtless discovered, it is one thing to conduct a lively lesson on money management, but something else to write about it. In writing, there is always the temptation to tell the obvious—which is, in itself, a great waste of words. Get in the *what* and *why* and *how-to-do;* weed out such statements as, "In buying a house, always look at the foundation." Pay the reader the compliment that he knows enough to do this, and use your words to tell what to look for in examining that foundation.

Rather than to use meaningless expressions as, "One's clothing dollars should be spent intelligently," expand the thought; be specific. If an obvious statement of fact must be made, try to give it a new twist—as in the discussion of the dollar at the beginning of this chapter. These are the things that help to make your writing stand up and stand for something of value to the consumers who read what you have to say. ●

CHAPTERETTE: *Adding Showmanship to Static Displays*

ONE AID to visual presentations about which little has been written is the window display—space built along the inside corridors of many schools.

In several ways these correspond to store and shop windows, so the following suggestions from a professional window dresser may help. He says:

- While in any display there must be one central idea, it should be supplemented by a number of supporting accessories. Why? Because it is not enough merely to call attention to an idea; it must invite studied observation.
- In every display one color (or combination of colors) must predominate so that the passerby gets the impression that this is, for example, a pink window or a bold splash of pinks and purples. When the predominant color coincides with whatever one is currently in vogue, the effect will be remembered.
- If the display needs a headline or sales line to drive home the basic idea, dramatize it in some way. Examples: You might cover the floor area with a bright-colored plastic tablecloth and on it write the message boldly, using a felt-tipped pen. . . . Or in a display of old-fashioned garments you might make a cardboard facsimile of a huge sampler and hang it against the background. Use old-fashioned "sampler" script to write the tag line. ●

Ask yourself, "What do I want this display to say?" When you define your problem, the solution is almost sure to be forthcoming.

11. INTRODUCING HOMEMAKING TO *Little Children*

Give a little girl a taste of homemaking, then watch her appetite for it increase with the years.

WHATEVER your home economics category, you are concerned directly or indirectly with child care and development. Not only because you are interested in the welfare of children generally, but because you realize they will shape the world of tomorrow. And if you know any little folks personally, it is quite likely that, at times, you introduce them to some of the satisfactions and fun that go with homemaking.

Perhaps you equip their sandbox with measuring cups and spoons, and small-sized flour sifters and cake pans, in order that they may get the feel of these useful household tools. Possibly you stir up a good, durable cooky dough for them to use in place of modeling clay, then bake their edible ceramics. At times you invite them to join you in making pancakes or puddings or peanut butter sandwiches. And surely you take them marketing occasionally and, at other times, make it easy for them to play at keeping store.

(Speaking of children and marketing: Hundreds of you are acquainted with Elena Zelayeta through her cookbooks, lectures, and demonstrations; perhaps have heard her tell how, in the early years of her blindness, she always took her three-year-old son, Billy, with her when she went to the corner grocery store. "Find Mother a can of tomatoes," she would say. And Billy would look among the canned foods until he found one with a picture of tomatoes on it. The grocer would gladly have helped Elena, as would any of the other shoppers, but she wanted Billy to learn that he must assume responsibility within his capabilities. And, of course, like any other three-year-old, Billy enjoyed "helping" his mother, and felt important doing so.)

There are so many things that anyone can do with and for a child with whom she is personally concerned. Much, too, that all home economists can do individually and collectively to extend and strengthen the prekindergarten movement in all communities. For example:

ONE TEACHER SAYS:

Children need to invent and create and become mentally aggressive. The earlier they acquire these habits, the better adjusted they will be.

- If you are free to do so and have the necessary teaching credentials, why not investigate the possibilities of doing part-time or full-time teaching in such schools. With the inauguration of the "Head Start" project, many more teachers and teacher aids are needed to carry out the program.

- In preparing recipe leaflets, surely you can tuck in an occasional recipe that children will enjoy trying by themselves or "helping" their mothers put together.

BOXES, BOXES, BOXES

A cardboard carton is a wonderful toy. It can be a doll house; a garage; a cage for a roaring toy lion; a table; a trailer to be dragged behind a tricycle or toy automobile. Several together can make a train, a store, a high-rise apartment.

- If you have an analytical mind, you might well study current television programs designed to interest and/or entertain children. Many program planners welcome outside comments, constructive criticism, and concrete ideas.

- When you see a display of how-to books for children, look them over to see what is in-

Play

cluded on homemaking. Remind publishers of the need and opportunity to work in occasional references to household tasks, as, "John is sorting and matching the socks as they come from the drier."

DO TOUCH

Children need to see, to feel, and to handle things. Looking at pictures of things is not quite enough to satisfy their curiosity.

• If you have writing skills, you might well contact the manager of some food market chain to see if he might not sponsor a "Buy-and-Cook Book" for primary grade children. As any publisher will tell you, cookbooks for children are not always good sellers. But a book that tied together buying and cooking might well be one of the most constructive steps ever taken in consumer education. And you could be the one to write it.

Ways

• If you are a member of the projects committee for your local home economics group, you might consider preparing a mimeographed sheet of helps for baby sitters, to be distributed through local home economics teachers.

The possibilities for such activities are many. These suggestions are merely to start you thinking along that line.

WHAT IS A GOOD KINDERGARTEN?

N.E.A. recommends that in all kindergartens there should be introductory lessons in science, language, math, art, health education, and citizenship. Shouldn't homemaking be included? Surely every child is entitled to be introduced to it!

HISTORY NOTE

The kindergarten movement preceded the founding of home economics by almost half a century. As early as the 1850's there were kindergartens in this country, all based on the theories

Educators are finding that many of the school failures so common among disadvantaged children stem not from a lack of brains, but from a lack of stimulation in their early years.

of Friedrich Froebel in Germany. By 1880 the movement had spread to every major city in the nation. During the late 1890's Mrs. Ellen Richards, chemist, together with a group of associates began laying the groundwork of home economics in the United States, and by 1900 the movement was well under way. Simultaneously, Rachel and Margaret McMillan, teachers, were fostering their nursery schools in England, and Mme. Maria Montessori, a doctor of medicine, was establishing her first child-care centers in Rome. All of these pioneering women had one thing in common: *Vision.*

Mme. Montessori, concerned primarily with the health and development of disadvantaged children, believed that even the smallest child could and should develop skills. The McMillan sisters were convinced that children should be permitted to grow and expand in happy surroundings. Mrs. Richards felt strongly that domestic activities should be elevated to a status far different from that of her own childhood in New England. She wanted genuine, broad, but home-centered education for girls, not mere training in domestic skills. And so, while each of these pioneers had her own goals, each in her own way was working constructively toward better family living.

QUESTIONNAIRE

How many prekindergarten children do you know?

How long since you have peeked into a nursery school?

Have you recently spent an hour trying to amuse a small child, or an older one?

Do you know what provision is made in your community for taking care of children of working mothers?

You may be asking, "What has all of this to do with bringing homemaking information to life —which is the thesis of this book?" The answer lies in one word: *Communications.*

Dr. Montessori's ideas and ideals became known to the world largely through the writings of Dorothy Canfield Fisher. Nursery schools as we know them today in this country came about because the McMillan sisters had written a book which served as a pattern for the establishment of such schools. And Mrs. Richards and her colleagues knew how to make words work for their cause. Otherwise home economics might have died aborning.

It is interesting to note that in all of the writing for and about those early day movements, a genuine enthusiasm shone through between the lines. There was a crusading spirit about them that gave strength and vitality to the copy. Might it be that more of those same qualities are needed in today's home economics communications? It's a thought! ●

FROEBEL'S THEORY

Friedrich Froebel, founder of the first kindergarten, based his theory on the idea that child training should be a development from within, never a prescription from without.

12.

DEVELOPING MORE EFFECTIVE *Bulletin Boards* AND *Posters*

There should be more to a wall display than first meets the eye. Ingenuity can put it there.

WHEN bulletin boards, flannel boards, posters, and wall charts hang side by side, you can easily recognize their differences and their likenesses.

Strictly speaking, a *bulletin board* is simply a stationary board for displaying notices, bulletins, announcements, and items of news or special importance. In classroom usage, however, the bulletin board usually means a special display space where ideas or bits of information can be highlighted in an interesting way.

As the name suggests, *flannel boards* are of flannel to which materials and light objects easily adhere. (Various relatives of the flannel board, such as Velcro boards, are becoming popular; they are basically the same. Both are useful as demonstration devices and for exhibits.)

Posters are colorful paper placards stressing a specific idea or making an announcement in a bold, artistic way.

A *chart*, according to the dictionary, is a "sheet exhibiting information in tabulated or methodical form." Some so-called wall charts should really be called posters because they are primarily pictorials rather than tabulations.

All such displays regardless of differences in form and in terminology have a number of things in common. Each one must attract attention through color, design, and wording. It must get across a definite idea quickly and in a way that makes it remembered. It must have a center of interest. It should be placed at eye level. Materials (or media) used should, whenever feasible, be in harmony with the subject matter. And in the case of bulletin boards, a third dimension should be added whenever it is sensible to do so. (The visual at the end of this chapter shows one interesting way to add that extra dimension.)

HARMONY

Bulletin boards should be in harmony with the colors and architecture of the room. If the room is modern in feeling, the displays should reflect that same effect.

LAYOUT

The layout of any bulletin board or poster can be made more effective if tested in roughed-out forms. By helping, students learn the importance of such planning in all types of presentations.

DEVELOPING A FILE OF BULLETIN BOARD DISPLAYS

Undoubtedly you keep a file of ideas that might be used in, or adapted to, bulletin board displays. The reminders included here are designed to be added to just such lists.

For Backgrounds. Fabrics (as felt or burlap) in attractive colors; construction paper; gift-wrapping paper; colorful tissue paper fastened down securely so that it does not wrinkle; Saran over tissue paper; straw place mats fitted close together so that they cover the board; small-figured wallpaper with a big patch of harmonious construction paper imposed on it to hold the message and illustration; peg board; plastic-coated screening; embossed tablecloth—to mention a few.

ADDED DIMENSION

Bits of bark, sponge, corrugated cardboard, sandpaper, and the like can contribute interesting texture and depth to a bulletin board; especially when cut into unusual or geometric shapes.

For Lines (leading from one area of visual to another). Yarn; crocheted cord; fine wire; zipper; tape measure; ribbon; finishing tape; paper chain; lightweight metal chain (available in hardware stores); grains of rice, wheat, corn, or decorative seeds.

BULLETIN-BOARD PEOPLE

Lifelike and amusing figures made from pipe cleaners, bent wire, sticks, and the like should suggest action. The less static, the more dramatic—always!

EXCHANGE

Is it feasible for neighboring schools to exchange bulletin boards and posters? Is it sensible to take a snapshot of each bulletin board as it appears—and then, at year's end, compare them?

KING-SIZED POSTER

Christmas exhibit or open house coming up? How about you letting (which means encouraging) students do a floor-to-ceiling poster of a Christmas tree, using crayon or paints? Title it "Home for Christmas." On tree hang colorful cutouts of useful gifts for the home: scissors, measuring cups or spoons, skillets, a clock, etc. Have a step stool nearby so that girls can more easily distribute the "gifts."

MATERIAL FOR SAME

If possible, get extra-wide paper for the project suggested above; it's much simpler than trying to piece together sheets of narrow paper. Check with commercial photographers or display houses. It is available, but you may have to hunt for it.

PERSONAL FROM AUTHORS

A king-sized poster such as described was the main feature of an HEIB Christmas party in San Francisco. Each guest drew a free-hand bauble on the tree, and signed her name to it.

For Pointers (attached to cut-out paper hand that points to the slogan). Knitting needle; ruler or yardstick; pencil; drinking straw; skewer; wooden spoon; bamboo stick; chopsticks; tall slender taper; or line of push pins or thumbtacks placed close together.

For Lettering. Wax pencil; felt-tipped pen; poster paint; crayon; colored chalk; fingernail polish; push pin letters or figures (obtainable from school supply or library supply houses); plastic house numbers; anagrams; and the like. One resourceful business home economist likes to paint the letters of a caption with white glue (such as Elmer's), then carefully sprinkle colored sugar over the glue before it sets.

To Hold Items in Place on Board. Use glue or paste; double-stick tape; corsage pins or ornamental hat pins, strategically placed; various materials backed with sandpaper for use on flannel board; push pins or tacks carefully concealed or used with emphasis such as a thumbtack might be stuck into the ring finger of a paper hand to suggest a jewel set in a ring. Rather than paste directly onto corkboard background, you will, of course, cover board with some sort of removable material.

Useful Accessories and "Building Materials." Tongue depressors; plastic berry baskets (to make tiny tennis racquets, for example); artificial daisies and fern fronds; paper plates, cups, and spoons; buttons; bits of cloth; stage money; sea shells; empty eggshells (whole, or lengthwise halves); beads; purse mirrors; fans; little rag dolls or plastic dolls; doll clothes; plastic "pill containers" from drugstore; foil; clear plastic wrap—almost any "clamjamfry."

Geometric Figures. Patterns of circles, squares, triangles, rectangles, and the like. For example: A *circle* can easily become a ball; a balloon; an apple or peach or orange; a head of cabbage or lettuce; a cake, a pie, or a cooky; a pumpkin; a clock; a flower; a flower bowl; an old-time cooking pot or skillet; a banjo; a bubble light; a bridal bouquet; the world. *Two small circles* can make a pair of sun glasses; or wheels on a bicycle. A *half-circle* easily turns into a bowl; a parasol; a hat; a segment of it can be the new moon. *Two half-circles* can make a butterfly. A *square* can be a building block; a mortar board. A *rectangle* can represent a room; a bookcase; a refrigerator; a window; a table mat; a menu; a book. A *triangle* immediately suggests a tree; a sailboat; a tent; the crown of a sombrero; a birdhouse; a skirt. And so on and on.

Imagination can dramatize information, reminding us that it is awareness plus creativity plus the process of reasoning which activate the yeast that leavens all learning. ●

FRAME UP

When students run out of ideas for the bulletin board, suggest that they work up a temporary frame for the board—perhaps a rococo one cut from cardboard and decorated with paints. Once the frame is done, some one of the girls will have come up with an idea of a display to put inside it!

Here a piece of construction paper has been folded and slipped over the crossbar of a wire coat hanger. On the top panel has been pasted (or drawn) an illustration of a coat. On bottom panel is an illustration of a dress that would be suitable to wear under such a coat. Caption goes on bottom panel which is slightly long than top piece. Hanger can be painted to match construction paper.

CHAPTERETTE: *Adapting Cartoon and Animation Techniques*

THINK BIG

Encourage students to prepare oversized visuals occasionally. For example, giant sunflowers with paper-plate centers and frilly petals cut from construction paper. Use thin plant stakes for stems.

Take advantage of fads and trends in planning poster displays. For example, if the vogue is for some color, or for using gaudy peacock feathers, or crewel embroidery, or some new color in room decor, use them on the board in some way, then let class evaluate them. Makes for judgment.

Amateur art in cartoons and animations must be kept extremely simple. Wording should be reduced to a minimum.

SINCE CARTOONS AND ANIMATIONS are very much a part of today's communications, students usually enjoy seeing them worked into bulletin boards, chalk talks, filmstrips, and other teaching aids. This is easier to do than one might imagine. Here is how it works out:

There is to be a meeting of importance and a quick-to-make sign is needed. You suggest the line, "Your Golden Opportunity," and challenge students to introduce animation. They come up, perhaps, with a floppy goldfish cut from gilt paper, and draw a fish bowl around him. From his mouth comes a bubble bearing the message.

Or you want to emphasize the importance of reading fine print in a contract or other legal paper. On bottom of bulletin board or on a card you mount a legal form, with pen in place ready to sign on the dotted line. Now you bring it to life with animation—for instance a wise old owl saying, "Wait. Read that fine print!" Make the words "fine print" as small as possible.

Or a poster is needed to emphasize the correct cooking of vegetables in order to conserve vitamins and minerals. Obviously such a poster cannot be made to apply to all vegetables, so you concentrate on the quickly cooked ones. You begin by drawing ears of corn, stalks of asparagus, heads of cabbage, and such. Then you decide to turn them into "little people" with a few strokes of pen, pencil, or brush. With that for a start, it is only a step to lining them up as in a protest march, with the figures carrying signs reading, "Don't overcook me." "I demand brief cooking." And so on.

Why emphasize this phase of communication? Answer: Writing tag lines for cartoon sketches helps one to understand the value of a crisp topic sentence. Animating items or animals develops imagination—brings out hidden talent. Exploring new avenues of expression makes communication more challenging. ●

13.

MAKE-AS-YOU-GO GRAPHICS FOR *Chalk Boards* AND *Projectors*

EVERY TYPE of visual aid has its place in today's show-and-tell system of learning. But there is something about make-as-you-go graphics, done on the chalk board or for an overhead projector, that seems to give them a reality and effectiveness all their own. Whether you write with chalk on a chalk board, or with a special pencil on the writing roll of a projector, students profit by seeing an idea come into life before their eyes, just as a child is fascinated by watching from start to finish as his mother makes and frosts a cake.

Simplest way to get across an idea on chalk board or projector is, of course, to tie it in with a symbol. For example, in presenting a lesson on meal planning, you might write the four basic food groups on the board or writing roll. Instead of listing them in the usual way, however, you use them as boundaries on a square, and, after discussion, put the menu or meal plan into that square.

You will find many such ideas in this book. While they are suggested for chalk board presentation, all are adaptable to mechanical production as well.

For a chalk board that all can see, there is the overhead projector to tell your story.
Make the most of it.

Overhead projectors do, of course, have many advantages that the chalk board lacks: teacher faces students; time is conserved; color can be used; and, most important, every student can see and read what is going on. That old familiar chalk board does, however, still have its place in dramatizing and emphasizing facts, especially for small groups and for spur-of-the-moment thoughts. That is, the teacher, standing in any part of the room, may walk over to the board and write down a word or sentence or do a bit of chalk doodling that makes an idea spring to life.

First requirement for good communications is that you have something of worth to communicate.

For example, in a personal development class, you are discussing charm. On a chalk board you might spell the word out as:

C ourtesy at all times; consideration of others.
H appy outlook on life; helpfulness.
A lways well groomed.
R egard for the rules on which a good society is built.
M anners based on thoughtfulness.

While this type of thing is a natural for the chalk board, it might not be quite so appropriate for screen projection.

COLOR COUNTS

The new method of teaching children to read by using color to represent sounds can be applied to nutrition teaching. Example: In listing foods on the board or in a meal-planning lesson, underscore protein-rich foods with red chalk (memory key—red for meat, etc.); vitamin-rich foods with green (key—green for vegetables); and so on.

Whenever you write or do informal "art" before a class, keep your wordage at a minimum. Also, do not strive for perfection in drawing those symbols, as the quality of imperfection actually heightens their appeal, makes them seem more direct and intimate. If you are not a good penman, you will undoubtedly letter your message. In either case, you will (it is hoped) be positive, not tentative. On the chalk board, make your writing or lettering large and bold; on the writing roll, size is unimportant because the copy will be blown up on the screen.

GIVE YOUR GRAPHICS A PERMANENT FINISH

One of the problems in many visual presentations is to keep them from going in one eye and out the other. Mechanical move-along can be so swift that it may not break through into the complete consciousness of every student. Your job, at times, is to slow down the presentation—let it sink in. As well you know, there are any number of ways to do this.

One long-established system is to set forth the visualized fact at the beginning of the class period, and then pick it up again at the end of the lesson. When using the chalk board, what you write at the beginning stays there through the period. When using the projector, the message is lost unless it is rewritten at the end. In either case, students have an opportunity to make notes.

A simple "gimmick" such as one of the following is also effective: On chalk board or writing roll, make a rough sketch of a hand. Write a headline: "Five Points To Remember." Under that heading list the five main points. In the discussion, encourage students to associate each point with a finger on one hand. Then erase everything except the drawing of the hand and the heading, and test to see how many of those five points the students can bring to mind.

Since every girl is familiar with getting "perms" for her hair, it sometimes helps in memorizing needed facts to present them as "getting a mind permanent"! Put down any set of basic facts, such as number of teaspoons or tablespoons in a standard measuring cup. Have students concentrate on list for a few seconds while their "perm" sets. At end of the period, check to see how the perm is holding up; check it again on another day. This is just one of those light con-

DRAW AND PASTE ON

For a nutrition graphic, draw a large square on sheet of cardboard. In it list the principal foods in each of the basic food groups. After discussion, turn square into a house. How? Have ready a square of equal size cut from colored construction paper. Tip it in place with gummed tape. Chalk in windows and door. Draw a peaked roof. Write, "Welcome to the House of Good Health."

NEWSPRINT PADS

Large pads of paper are often preferred to chalk boards or charts for sales meetings. If you cannot get the pads from a paper company, check with your local newspaper. Some editorial departments will have them made up for you.

FLIP CHARTS

For flip charts use a good quality of plastic-coated paper stock that will not crack in rolling. You can usually obtain it from any firm that deals in paper.

versation pieces that students seem to respond to. Any number of similar ones can be devised.

The point is this: Along with figuring how to make ideas and information come to life, you frequently need to go a step further in order to make them stick. When you do this, you give your visuals permanent visibility. Which is, of course, the aim of all visual education.

Whenever and wherever you use a mechanical visual device it is well to remember that while such aids may be perfect as machines, they can never substitute for human thought and personal interest. Just as the pioneer teacher writing on her blackboard was master of the chalk, so must the home economist of today be in control of mechanical aids. She must feed into them her own thinking and planning and enthusiasm if they are to project what is worthwhile and of lasting value. As you well know, the process of concentrated thinking is just plain hard work. But as you also know, the results of it are most gratifying. ●

MAGNETIC BOARDS

Magnetic chalk boards offer good possibilities for graphics, in that along with the chalk talks there can be clip-ons.

AUTHORS' NOTE

Are you one of the many home economists who has sat in on one of our workshops in home economics communications? If you are, you will recall the following chalk board graphic, which is actually the basis of our book How To Write for Homemakers, *Iowa State University Press, Ames, 1962.*

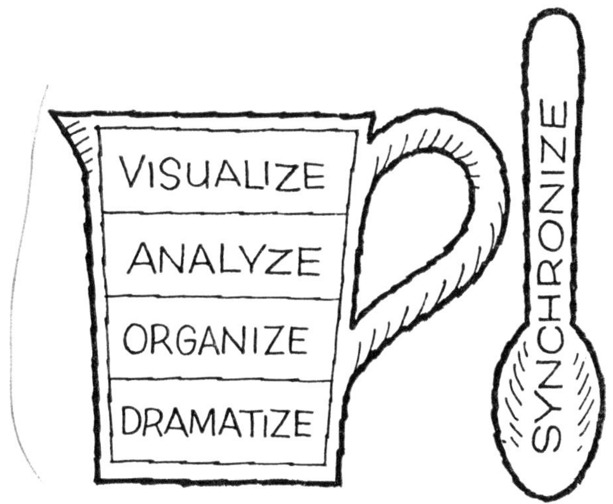

Why has this seemingly spontaneous visual been so easy to remember? There are four reasons: (1) It combines meaningful words with symbols related to homemaking—i.e., the measuring cup and spoon. (2) The measures on the cup make an automatic outline of those four key words: Visualize; Analyze; Organize; Dramatize. (3) That measuring cup, along with the spoon, suggests putting the formula to work. (4) And, most important of all, the visual gets right down to the heart of the subject matter.

Not all of the visuals we conceive live up to this standard. But getting at the essence of fact is the thing we work always to achieve. And who has taught us to do that? You who teach! For this, we thank you.

COVER UP

Idea: Prepare a part of your chalk board presentation in advance and cover it. As lesson comes to life with chalk talk, remove cover so that the whole story is revealed. The cover could be a sheet of construction paper gum-taped to top of board, or might be a cloth curtain on taut cord strung at top of board. Whatever the cover, keep at least half the area open for elaborating on the predrawn visual.

14.

HOW *Photographs* AND *Words* BOLSTER EACH OTHER

WHEN SOMEONE SAYS, "A picture is worth a thousand words," what is your reaction? Do you take the statement for granted? Or do you qualify it by saying, "Well, a *good* picture *might* be worth a thousand words, but that saying was coined a long time ago when pictorial reproductions were comparatively rare. It may or may not be true today."

Or do you reason something like this: *Most pictures need words to bring them to fullest reality; words usually take on greater importance with meaningful illustrations. What is needed is stronger hookup between the two.*

All pictures must speak for themselves. But they usually need to be reinforced with words.

If this is your thinking, it is in line with the belief of many educators and editors that a new dimension in communications can emerge from combining words and pictures in forceful ways and in ways that represent fresh thinking. As an example, they cite the television commercial.

You may disapprove of many television commercials being aired today, feeling that the end results do not justify the means employed. Nevertheless, the fact remains that most televised commercials do succeed in getting points across quickly in a way that makes them remembered. How is this accomplished? By skillfully combining words with pictured action—a technique that might well be adapted to home economics communications in general.

SHOW vs. TELL

When you want to present an idea to your boss, don't tell him about it—show him somehow what you have in mind. If it's a new plate arrangement for restaurant service, do a mockup of the plate... If it's a leaflet, show him your rough dummy. Often a snapshot can be made to tell a story, get across an idea.

MAKING YOUR PICTURES TALK

Adaptations of these theories are unlimited—here are two possibilities.

Situation. As a business home economist, a part of your work is to plan and prepare, for use on food pages of metropolitan newspapers, recipe releases with illustrative photographs. Let's say that the product you are concerned with is sugar, flour, or shortening, or raisins—something connected with baking.

Acting on a hunch, you have recently discovered that many recipes for drop cookies work equally well for making cupcakes. You have never heard of that idea or seen it in print, so you figure it has real news value and would appeal to food editors and their readers.

Before you give any thought to a photograph, however, you work on a headline for your idea—something like "Cookies and/or Cupcakes from the Same Dough." Once you have that headline, the simple photograph dictates itself—puffy cookies on one rack, attractive cupcakes on another, and an interesting mixing bowl (presumably one that has held the dough) disappearing in the background. Now you need only a caption for that photograph and a brief introductory paragraph for your recipe with its 2-way directions for baking, and your newsworthy recipe and picture are ready to be offered to editors.

Situation. You are planning an educational filmstrip. If you are an amateur, you are likely to start your thinking with photographic setups that might be made. But if you are an "old pro" you will think first in terms of words, sewing up your aim or principal thought into a headline which will be the title for the film. And when you get down to planning the individual frames, you will think of what the captions might be before you finalize the pictures.

MAKING FILMSTRIPS AND SLIDES

Main problem of the home economist is to realize that each frame (i.e., picture) must be set up in a small area. This means condensing your thinking to a sharp basic idea that requires a minimum of props to execute.

Words Are Important

Even though you think of your filmstrip pictorially—and you certainly must do that—do not underestimate the words that must support and supplement those pictures. Never expect any series of photographs, no matter how beautifully done, to carry the entire load. A caption for each frame, a commentary which the teacher reads or puts into her own words, are needed in order to give deeper meaning to the pictures.

But don't stop there. Try for new effects, new effectiveness with words. For example, why not insert an occasional nonpictorial frame which, in type, calls special attention to the following picture, or briefly explains a change in thought or subject matter? Such an interruption in a series of smooth-running pictures helps to bring the daydreaming student or homemaker back to reality; makes her follow the film more closely.

Make your words and pictures work together with power and precision. Think of them as a pair of skis: if one ski goes one way, and the other shoots off in another direction, there's trouble ahead. But when the two travel straight and smooth toward their destination, it shows that the skier is indeed master of his skis.

SLIDE SHOWS

How you use slides is even more important than the slides themselves. Don't be afraid to eliminate all mediocre frames—the audience will never miss them. Keep the narration brief and brisk—the picture must tell the story.

If a slide must be held longer than 20 to 30 seconds in order to be understood, you need another frame on the same subject.

Don't try to cover two ideas with one photograph.

WHEN YOU WORK ON PHOTOGRAPHS

In preparing any and all types of photographic illustrations, you, the home economist, are an interpreter. That is, your picture plus caption or body copy must interpret an idea. In working with a photographer or art director, you *interpret* to him the reasoning behind the picture, what you want to get across in it—and then leave the technical details to those graphic artists who see the problem through the eye of the camera. When the photograph you have selected is to appear in print, you write for it a meaningful caption that will *interpret* the picture more clearly to the readers. If your pictures are to be used as teaching aids, you interpret your ideas in ways that students can understand.

Before you can do an intelligent job of such interpretation, however, you must know something of the homemakers and future homemakers who will be attracted to your pictorial productions. You must understand editors and their editorial requirements. And before you work on photographic material designed for use in teaching, you certainly must have first-hand advice from home economics supervisors as to what is or is not acceptable. In brief, if you are on the producing side of photographs in any capacity, you are one link in a vast communications system. Think of yourself as just that.

LIGHTING

When using slides or a filmstrip, it usually is better to have some light in the room. Not so bright as to wash out or diminish the screen image.

BOOKS THAT HELP

Check with the Sales Service Dept. of Eastman Kodak Company, Rochester, N.Y., for a list of available books on color photography, indoors and out.

WHEN YOU WRITE CAPTIONS

The caption is an important element in any photographic illustration, and especially in those that relate to homemaking information. There is sometimes a tendency, however, to treat those lines or small blocks of descriptive copy rather

FILINGS

Keep a scrap file of setups that appeal to you. But keep it up to date. Styles in photography change as do styles in everything else. Even in words!

lightly, instead of using them to get at the heart of the idea that is being portrayed. It is well to remember that the word "caption" comes from the Latin word *caput,* meaning head, thus a caption is literally a "headline."

CLASSROOM MOVIES

If you have an interest in photography, make-your-own movies is an interesting experiment. Photograph students at work. At year's end cut and splice film to make a smooth-running review of the year's activities.

Many artists and art editors frown on the one-line caption under an illustration. They contend that those printed words look like "fringe." Others consider such lines largely as "fringe benefits." Regardless of how those captions appear in print, your job is to put meaning into them. If the illustration is in black and white, let the caption put color into the picture. If it is in color, use the caption to amplify the thought. But in no case should the caption merely parrot what has already been said in the body copy.

Give special thought to the captions—make them come to life with fresh wording.

Make the Caption Fit the Space

In writing a caption to fit space (as in following a layout, or writing captions for slides) you must, of course, count characters in order to make your words fill the allotted space exactly. In writing captions for pictures that are to be released to editors, you can go into detail without regard to word count, knowing that the editor will undoubtedly rewrite your caption to fit the space that is allowed for it.

Not every home economist who works with words and pictures is permitted to decide the exact format in which they are to be combined. Even so, it is interesting and helpful to study some of the caption devices that are in use today. Along with looking at the visual examples that follow, study current magazines and booklets for interesting and unusual ways of combining words with photographic illustrations. The possibilities are almost endless. ●

FOR YOUR IDEA FILE

• If you work with slides—particularly without the aid of specialists—you will find much of help in Service Pamphlet S-22, "Effective Lecture Slides," prepared by the Sales Division of Eastman Kodak Company, Rochester, N.Y. 14650. Single copies are free; a small charge is made for quantity lots.

• If you are concerned in any way with the production of business films, read or reread the article, "Lights, Art, Camera. Business Is the Star," that appeared in *Business Week*, May 29, 1965. A file of the magazine probably is in your local library.

• If you have a big supply of props and accessories to use in setting up food photographs, have them photographed and labeled as to color and size of dish, when and how used previously, etc. (Several pieces can be grouped together in one picture.) Such a file saves looking through cupboards and storage areas for a just-right accessory or background material.

• If your interest, photographically, is clothing or home furnishing, keep a special notebook of ideas from store window displays. Make special note of the lettered signs that accompany the displays. Those telling and selling words may prove helpful in writing future captions.

• If you work on food photographs, develop the kind of mind that enables you to make mental notes every time you walk through a department store or market or visit an art show or community fair. Remember: awareness + imagination + skills + the ability to put words into pictures and pictures into words is the key to success in all pictorial communications.

TIMING

As everyone in show business knows, timing is one of the most important elements in all showmanship.

Creative thinking plus the discipline to bring one's ideas down to practicality result in a truly fresh approach to home economics communications.

AUTHORS' NOTE

In the latest edition of our book, How To Write for Homemakers *(The Iowa State University Press, Ames, 1962), the subject of Photography and Art has been explored in detail. This chapter is an extension and expansion of that information.*

Illustrations

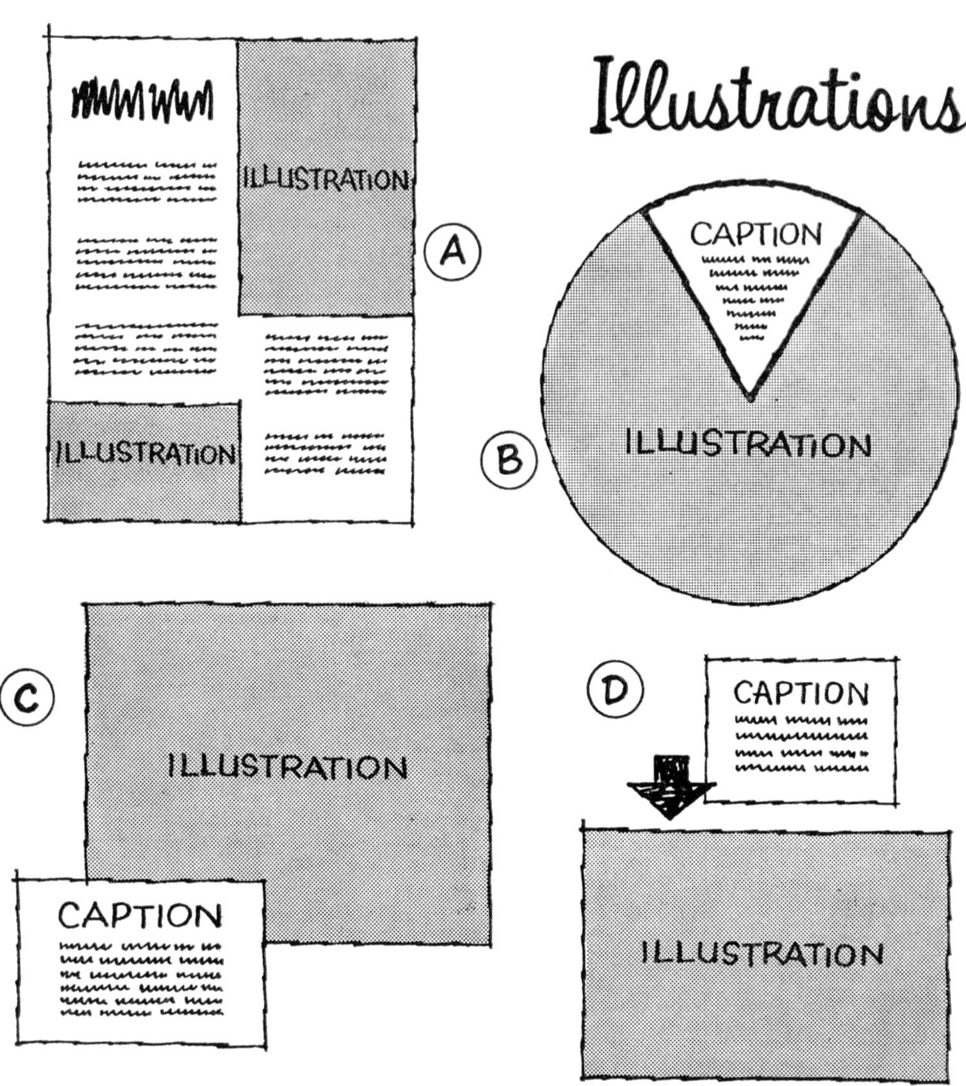

(**A**) Here, instead of featuring one caption per picture, body copy has been omitted and the space used for definitive block captions, each emphasizing some specific point. (**B**) The illustration is of a pie, one piece of which has been cut out to make room for caption. (**C**) Caption cuts into illustration—a good device in a photograph of a room, since the cut-in helps to kill floor space. (**D**) Caption is an overlay to be used in opaque projector.

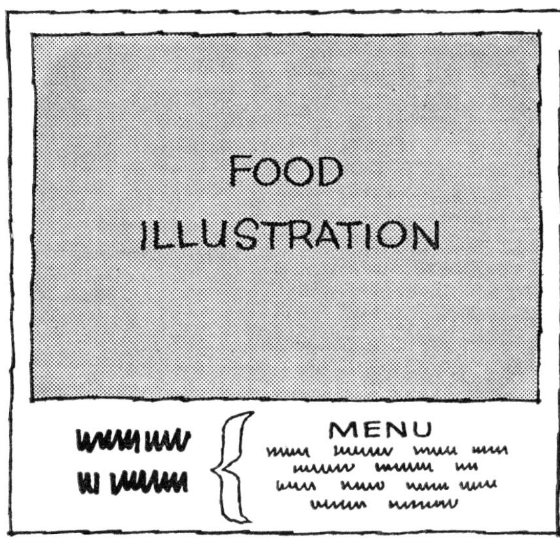

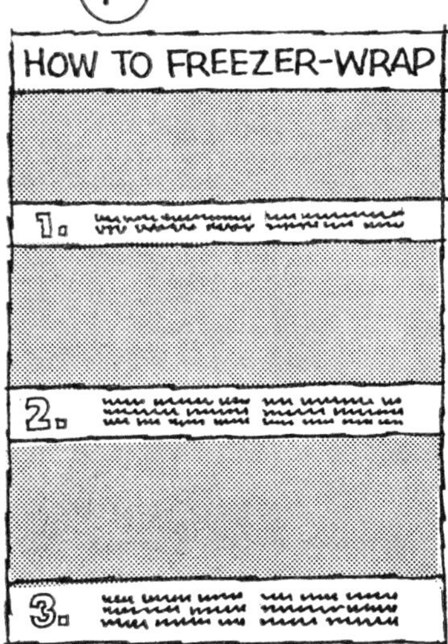

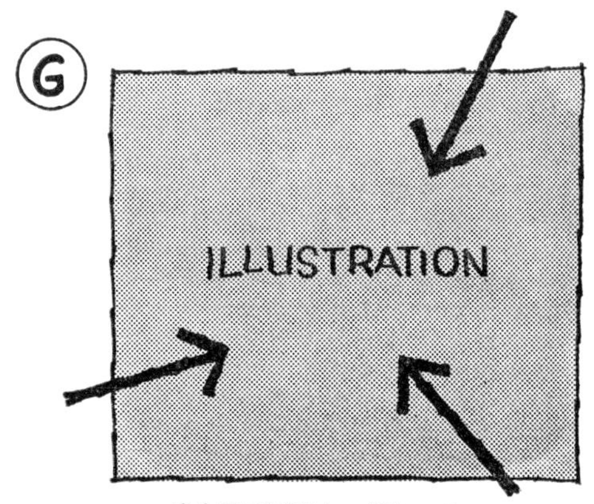

(E) A good caption device for a food illustration. It consists of a heading plus menu so that reader sees not only the pictured dish but what to serve with it. **(F)** In step-by-step illustrations, it is a good idea to start each caption with the verb denoting the action being performed. **(G)** In this illustration of a room, outstanding features are indicated by arrows super-imposed on the photograph or art work. The arrowed points are then further explained.

15.

THE 'JELLY-MAKING' SYSTEM OF *Writing*

WHEN you pick up your pencil to write a release or an article for a magazine, do your thoughts fly out the window? Do you find it difficult to make your words come alive; to make your sentences add up to something? If this is your problem, try comparing writing to the making of jelly. Since you know the principles involved in jelly making, all you need do is to proceed in much the same way. This is how it works out.

If writing is difficult for you, try this down-to-kitchen approach.

SQUEEZE YOUR THINKING

Having gathered and sorted your "fruit" (facts and ideas), the first step—in writing as in jelly making—is to extract the juice, get at the essence of your subject matter. Learn to squeeze your mind as you might squeeze a jelly bag, asking yourself over and over, "What am I really trying to say here? What is the one big idea I want to get across?" Keep squeezing and working until you can reduce your thinking to a single sentence. *That is your topic sentence!*

Once you have that topic sentence, you are ready to write. And not before. You may use it for your title or headline, or for your lead sentence. Or you may put it midway in your copy. *But that topic sentence must be there, and it must stand out—the essence of what you are to say.*

SHARPEN THE FLAVOR

After extracting the juice, what is the next step in making jelly? You add something. Sugar always to give it substance; sometimes a bit of lemon juice to bring out the natural flavor; sometimes a drop or two of coloring. In other words, you round it out. The same holds in writing—you expand that topic sentence and develop it just as good writers have through the centuries.

You simply cannot be a good writer unless you develop creativity and an inquiring mind. Too much writing today sounds regimented—no questioning of old ways.

When King David wrote the Psalms, he usually stated his topic sentence at once, as in the one that begins, "The Lord is my shepherd." In those five words David expressed the entire meaning of that psalm. But he then went on to expand his thought in word pictures which made his meaning completely clear and unforgettable.

There are thousands of just such examples in the wonderful world of words.

If you want to develop and strengthen your own writing skills, be topic-sentence conscious. Look for that important key sentence every time you read an item in a newspaper or an article in a magazine. You will find it usually in the first paragraph, frequently in the first sentence. And when you write anything, make sure your own topic sentence stands out. It's the thing that literally makes your writing "jell."

REMINDERS

Never say in writing or speaking that you are not an authority. Either be one or quote one . . . Anticipate readers' questions and answer them in advance . . . Avoid mental conflict with readers.

COOK CAREFULLY

Back again to the jelly making. The juice, sugar, and all are now ready to be cooked. Your topic sentence and ideas for developing it are in your mind, ready to be jelled into words. And so you concentrate on this crucial step. Boiling, stirring, timing, testing, guarding against boiling over —these have their obvious parallels in the job of writing. And you stay by your work, writing and rewriting, until you feel you have said what you wanted to say in a way that your readers will like. And then your "jelly" is done! That is, your copy is ready for the editor.

If you are an experienced jelly maker, you will have estimated how many glasses will be needed to hold that amount of jelly. If you are an experienced writer, you will have figured how much space your copy will occupy; or, what is more likely to be the case, you will be writing to a specific length. If, however, you are an amateur, you will be inclined to write along without regard for space, then try to cut or pad the copy to make it the right length. Such a procedure usually results in an awkward, patched-up piece of work.

MORE ABOUT WRITING AND JELLY MAKING

Most jelly needs skimming. So does most writing. If some of your precious words cloud the issue, have the courage to edit them out.

You can't make good jelly unless you give complete attention to it.

Synthetic flavor in writing is as easy to spot as synthetic flavor in jelly.

JELLY TEST

Just as a young cook finds it wise to call on an experienced jelly maker to look at that spoon test of her boiling jelly, so can the young home economist profit by asking her husband or someone else to read and evaluate what she has written.

JUDGING THE PRODUCT

The final test of a glass of jelly or a piece of copy comes later when the jelly is turned out of its glass or the copy is printed. Then and then only do you see whether or not it has held up and kept its sparkle. If good fruit has been used, if care is taken in the making, the jelly will go to the table triumphantly, and the writing will stand out on the printed page—firm but not hard, a pleasure to consume.

If you have ever judged jelly at a county fair, you know you allow so many points for clearness of product, so many for consistency, and so many for color and flavor. Your writing likewise is judged by those same qualities—clarity and con-

OLD-FASHIONED METHOD

Modern pectin products simplify the job of jelly making. But writing calls for the old-fashioned ingredients—good ideas and words—and is done with those old-fashioned tools: paper, pencil, and typewriter. Even tape-recorded copy must eventually be put into written words if it is to be published.

sistency, always, with something plus for colorful wording and lasting flavor.

There is, of course, more to writing than just the basic structure. Words, sentence balance, and the like are important, too. Consider them thoughtfully.

Look, too, at the authors' note which follows. It tells how, when, where, and why the "Jelly-making System of Writing" originated. ●

YOUR WRITING IS YOU

Whenever or whatever anyone writes, she gives herself away in it. If she is stiff and precise, her writing shows it. If she is nervous and excitable, her writing is wordy. If she is effusive and overenthusiastic chances are her writing is loaded with adjectives. If she is sharp-tongued, that feeling is almost certain to creep in. Frightening, isn't it?

AUTHORS' NOTE

This unorthodox approach to writing was first presented in expanded form as a talk to a group of home demonstration agents at an early breakfast meeting during their national convention in Chicago. In the 30 minutes allotted to the two of us, our assignment was to talk about writing.

Naturally, to condense so vast a subject into a few minutes' time called for concentration. Finally, by the weary process of thinking, it dawned on us that writing is much like making jelly in that the first and most important step in both is to extract the essence of the fruit or of the subject matter. As we worked on that thought, it became obvious that writing and jelly making had other similarities, and so the speech was evolved in that way.

Our talk was not a spectacular one, but it was direct and different, and had a freshness that seemed to be appreciated. And once more it became evident that likening an unfamiliar process to a familiar one can be a most useful device in either writing or speaking.

CHAPTERETTE: *Musical Visuals*

MUSIC AND STYLE SHOWS

Now that many style shows—in school and out—have turned into "dance shows," music with beat as well as melody must be considered.

SINCE HOMEMAKERS and homemakers-to-be do much of their homework against a background of music, it is only logical that music and musical themes are being made an integral part of more and more audio-visual programs.

Beginning in kindergarten, children are taught that there is music to be listened to and music to do things by. All of which is preparation not only for music appreciation, but for a need for music that seems to go with modern living.

Homemaking students, along with others, are now being tested as to whether they think more clearly or less clearly when there is music in the air: in sessions that have to do with family living, the effects of music in the home are frequent topics of discussion; business home economists are experimenting with using music to set the mood for demonstrations; teachers are taking advantage of musical signs and terminology to give importance to bulletin boards, posters, and school style shows.

A catalog that lists recordings is a good addition to the poster file. A quick glance through it will remind you of song titles around which posters and the like might be built.

For one example: Your junior high students are planning a nutrition poster. Since they seem to be fresh out of ideas, you mention that perhaps a musical thought might be introduced—as creating a character called "Maestro Milk." Students take the idea from there.

Or the subject is grooming and you suggest that they think in terms of song titles, old and new. "You Are My Sunshine," for example, prompts a poster based on care of skin and hair during the long, hot summer.

With such a start, it is surprising how enthusiastically students respond and how much ingenuity they display. To young people, music is a natural part of living—and those of any age without it find life rather flat. ●

16.

Picture-making Words

SPARK LIVELIER COPY

MUCH has been said in foregoing chapters about using pictorial words to produce "mental visuals" in the minds of readers or listeners. Sometimes, however, even better mental pictures can be projected by the skillful handling of words which are not in themselves pictorial. There are several possible ways of proceeding.

CREATE MENTAL PICTURES BY AMPLIFICATION

What's in a word? Everything — if it creates a clear mental picture for those who see or hear it.

The word "beautiful" is a pretty adjective, but in itself does not bring to mind any definite image. If, in the song "America the Beautiful," the author had merely said, "America is a beautiful land," she would have said nothing. But when she tells in what ways it is beautiful (for spacious skies, fields of grain, purple mountains, etc.) she makes a word picture that really sings.

When in writing or speaking, you state that a room is colorful, it means little unless you tell what colors predominate, and then amplify those colors—as watermelon pink; chalk white; teakwood brown—choosing adjectives that specify a particular shade or degree of that color. If, in the caption of a picture you say, "This costume is very smart," you have wasted your words unless you explain what makes it smart—good design, fineness of fabric, simplicity of line, or quality of workmanship. The words "drip-dry" conjure up a picture, but the picture is incomplete unless there is a statement as to whether or not the garment or curtain requires pressing. On the other hand, to speak of "drip-dry spareribs" gives a mental picture of spareribs cooked on some sort of rack so that the fat drips through.

When you say that a particular casserole or dessert fits well into a dinner for guests, it means little unless you pictorialize—say that it can be put together the day before, is easy to serve, and so on. That amplification gives the homemaker a picture of herself making that casserole or dessert to serve to her friends.

FIT WORDS TO SUBJECT MATTER

When you write about clothing and styles, use plenty of colorful and descriptive adjectives. When you write about housekeeping, be brisk and to the point. When you write about food, put fresh, appealing flavor into your words.

In all of your writing or speaking, work to amplify static words to give them action and quick visibility. Even when word space is limited, it is usually possible to do this. And certainly it is worth the effort!

PUT PICTURES INTO WORDS BY COMPARISONS AND CONTRASTS

Let us say that you are pointing up the value of eggs from the standpoint of nutrition and cost. When you make the general statement that eggs provide good nutrition at low cost, your words are likely to float in the air without alighting on anyone's mind. But when you explain that an egg at current prices costs about the same as two cups of coffee (brewed at home), yet supplies six to seven grams of protein, your words take on meaning. Then, if in discussing calories you say, "One medium egg (whole) has approximately 77 calories, or about half the calories found in a doughnut," you not only create a picture but plant a thought.

The pioneer woman who spoke of using "butter the size of a walnut," or said, "When the fat is hot enough to make little waves in the kettle, it is time to drop in the first doughnuts," she created pictures through comparison.

And so it is whenever you say that one thing is like or unlike another and in what ways. Try it. Not to excess, of course, but as an occasional change of pace.

IT'S A FACT

Man is known by the metaphors he uses. When you say, for example, "Some days it's just too wet to plow," you indicate your agricultural background.

GIVE VISIBILITY TO WORDS BY DEFINITION AND INTERPRETATION

In writing about food there sometimes is the tendency or temptation to use words that to some readers might seem vague or pretentious—such words as compote, gateau, ragout, sauté, julienne, and the like. These are acceptable to many audiences, but if you feel your audience might find them unfamiliar, explain them in a way that will not sound condescending: if you are speaking, spell them out; if writing, give the pronunciation, but use tact in your approach.

When you wish to emphasize a word that is commonly used, but not always completely understood in all of its ramifications, it is often helpful to analyze it. In discussing the word communications, for example, mentioning that the "*com*" means "together" helps to clarify not only the meaning of communications but of all words that begin with that prefix.

It is well, too, to consider words that are in common usage within the profession of home eco-

SOMETHING TO THINK ABOUT

Are recipes becoming so cut and dried that they discourage our using ingenuity and judgment? Study the ones you write; see if you can reword them so that they sound less didactic, more easy-going.

nomics, and make certain they are understood by the lay public. In your teaching, for example, you speak (naturally) of Clothing Courses, because you want to implant in students' minds that clothing means more than sewing. In talking with Mary's mother, however, you might very well say, "Mary has done so well in her sewing classes, I think she might eventually find work in the alterations department of a store." And then go on to mention that the courses in *clothing* help a girl to fit herself for such opportunities.

In other words, language is for the people. The more effectively you can interpret it, the better you can reach and teach your audience.

WORD CHALLENGE

Go through any professional article. Ask yourself, "If *Readers' Digest* were to reprint this, what words and phrases would its editors cross out?"

TAKE ADVANTAGE OF DEFINITIVE AND INVENTED WORDS

If you hope to plant exact images, use precise words. Hunt for the right verb! In a recipe, for example, decide whether the word should be "mix" or "blend" or "stir" or "beat." Instead of using the word "add," ask yourself if it would not be more accurate to say "stir in" or "beat in." Look out for that word "place." Far too many recipes still call for doing such absurd things as "place a cup of water in a saucepan," or "place a can of tomato soup in a casserole," when what is meant is to *pour* the water into a saucepan, or *empty* the can of soup into the casserole!

QUOTE

The four most important phrases in management-worker relations are: "I am proud of you." "What is your opinion?" "If you please." And "Thank you." Least important word: "I."

Along with striving to find definitive words, try inventing new ones occasionally. Today's dictionary contains many words that were coined only a few years ago but have come into common usage. Teen-ager, cookout, housecoat, brunch are typical examples. See, too, what you can do in inventing words that relate to home economics. How about home-ability; cookcraft; sewmanship; skill-thrills; money-matics; Homelife Sciences;

Vita-video (meaning living visuals)? You can do better than these!

In all of your efforts to use just-right words, beware of overworking any word. In one single-page typewritten release about a forthcoming home economics meeting, the word "values" appeared 13 times. Any qualities the word might once have had were dulled by that repetition. A better approach would be to say, "The aim of this meeting is to get at the roots of three basic problems that are of concern to all home economists."

Be a word watcher. It is not only a stimulating hobby, but it is an integral part of good communications.

All political leaders know the value of using lines that become quotes or slogans. Example: "We have nothing to fear but fear itself." That same technique can apply to home-centered information. Example: "Think twice before you wave buy-buy at every pay check!"

TRY TO FIGURE OUT UNEXPECTED WORD PICTURES

It is interesting to analyze the success of Mark Twain as a writer and lecturer. Contrary to usual opinion, his appeal lay not so much in his humor as in his totally unexpected comments. They might be humorous, they might be serious, they might be descriptive, but they had freshness and the element of surprise that has made them memorable.

Mark Twain had no monopoly on that quality. The teacher (home economics or otherwise) who springs an eye-opening remark on her students is the one who wins attention and influences thought and action. The business home economist who injects fresh words and phrases into her demonstrations is the one that homemakers like to listen to and to watch. The cookbook author who punctuates her recipes with an occasional smile is the one whose book is read and treasured and used. Work for originality. You have more of it than you know.

It is not likely that you have ever panned

MORE ON DISCIPLINE

Undisciplined ideas are like undisciplined children—they get out of hand and cause trouble!

for gold, but you know the principle involved. The miner scoops up a pan of gravel, washes it, swishes it around, all the time scanning it for the yellow flecks that tell him traces of gold are present. Use a similar process in searching for pictorial and expressive words. It is hard work, but it can be exciting. And when you discover real nuggets, you know that your labor has not been in vain. ●

CHAPTERETTE: *Brief Commentary on Television*

IN A BOOK that has to do with dramatizing communications, television must be explored from a variety of angles.

When a number of established program planners were interviewed as to the place of home economics in television, these quotes were jotted down:

"Facts and ideas, even though important and interesting, are not enough to make a television program. There must be enough action, enough showmanship, to bring the material to life on the screen. Best results are obtained when the home economist or other expert is directed by persons who are experienced in television techniques."

"Home economists who work closely with a specific product frequently forget that the function of a television commercial is to 'sell'—not merely to show how to use."

"Many youth programs (panels, interviews, etc.) designed to reflect the opinions of young people can be strengthened by the unobtrusive guidance of teachers. Greater emphasis needs to be put on suggestions as to what might be done rather than on criticism of things-as-they-are. And all young people—whether chiefly interested in home economics or history, math or music—need much more and better training in good basic English and diction."

At the moment, the chief role of most home economists in television seems to be to work in the background, and let others appear and speak for them—meanwhile learning everything they can about this branch of communications. ●

AUTHORS' NOTE

Fresh ideas are not always—if ever—put in motion immediately. Example: In the *California Cookbook* (first published in '46) there appeared on page 169 a completely original recipe for a Mixed Bean Casserole. At the time this note is being written (1965) that casserole and various salads derived from the same idea, renamed, are being introduced in many parts of the country as brand new and highly popular.

CHILDREN AND TV

Many more television programs for children are in the planning stage than ever before. Problem is how to fit them in and around the child's other activities. Is there an answer to this?

17.

MORE 'COME-ON' FOR *Bulletins* AND *Leaflets*

A LOOK NOW at bulletins, booklets, leaflets, newsletters, and the like, and how to make them say, *"Come read me; I'm interesting."* In other words, how to put life into such printed publications. Although booklets, bulletins, leaflets, and newsletters are often spoken of collectively, each has its own function and, usually, its own format. Make that distinction within your own mind, and keep to it as you plan and write.

BULLETINS AND BOOKLETS ARE "LITTLE BOOKS"

In preparing a bulletin, you do, of course, have previous departmental bulletins to guide you, and you undoubtedly work closely with others in your department. If you arc the one responsible for the planning and writing, think that bulletin through for yourself! One good place to start is to analyze critically a number of bulletins that are similar in size and content to the one with which you are concerned.

Unless printed material has eye appeal, it may never be seen, much less read and heeded.

Test those bulletins, page by page, asking such questions as these:

Would more subheads have promoted easier readability?

YARDSTICK

Every bulletin, booklet, or leaflet should: look interesting; be interesting to read; have something in it that invites using and keeping.

Are those subheads too heavy, too light; would they have been better set in italics, or set in two lines, flush with the left hand of the body copy to give the impression of more air?

Would it have helped to have dropped in a few questions and answers for a change of pace, or underscored the words in some of the paragraphs?

Might it not have been better to have boxed three or four of the most important facts?

COVER "COME-ON"

Every booklet, bulletin, and leaflet needs a sharp cover. Keep it simple, make the title stand out, and work for clean-cut design rather than fussy artwork.

If boxes were used, study to see if there is enough white space around them, inside and outside.

Could the title of the bulletin have been more definitive?

And what about the art (if any); is it meaningful? (Since bulletins are built around solid information, meaningless art is inclined to weaken rather than strengthen.)

MAKE A DUMMY

ENLARGED VISION

In many cases it is worthwhile to "blow up" the cover of your booklet or leaflet to giant size for use on posters and in store displays. Size and dramatics are closely related.

After such analysis, try making a rough dummy of how your new bulletin might look. Next estimate the approximate number of words required. Then make an outline of all of the major facts that should be included. After all of this, you and your co-workers are ready to discuss what should be done, and how. You may decide that it might be better to concentrate on only one segment of the proposed subject rather than attempt to cover it completely. That is, instead of a bulletin on Food Freezing, you may reason that it might be advisable to limit the foods covered, devoting all of the space to the freezing of meats, game, and fish. Or reduce the subject still further to freezing game and fish.

Having a theme holds a booklet together.

When all are in agreement as to approach and format, you are ready to write. And this you must do in a live and interesting way. What you want to achieve is a bulletin that looks inviting, is easy to read, and is packed with helpful information.

Booklets, like bulletins, are usually approached as a group effort. In commercial booklets, however, there is likely to be more emphasis on art than in educational bulletins. Therefore, working closely with the artist is a part of your responsibility. He, rather than you, will be the one to make a dummy, but he will expect you to give him a rough idea of what you have in mind. He will want to know the type of material you are planning and, if possible, see some of the copy before he starts his thinking and planning. And you, in turn, will want to see his pencilled sketches ("roughs") to make sure that you, he, and others concerned are all working in the same direction.

A WARNING

Working out a clear, orderly outline is the first step in putting together any leaflet, booklet, bulletin, or other production. But don't stop there! Remember, an outline is a skeleton—the bony structure which gives shape and strength to the finished piece. Your job is to bring that outline to life by converting those main points and subpoints into sentences and paragraphs that have life and color and meaning and personal appeal. The outline must be there, underneath, but its "bones" must not show!

LEAFLETS CALL FOR SPECIAL TECHNIQUES

Where do you start in preparing a leaflet? Usually by bringing your ideas down into actual page size. (Remember, the word "leaflet" means, literally, a "little leaf," i.e., a little page.) Here, again, begin your thinking by visualizing those small pages and figuring how to pack them with eye appeal.

Since homemakers are inclined to connect leaflets with recipe material, it is a good idea to give your leaflet a recipe look, regardless of the subject matter. That is, break up those little panels or pages with subheads—give the feeling of a great many good ideas packed in small space, but not crowded.

DISTRIBUTION

If your piece is to be mailed out, give thought to the envelope before you decide on the size of the booklet. The standard size is least expensive. Figure, too, what you can do to add interest and sales appeal to the envelope.

Use plenty of originality and ingenuity. In a food leaflet, consider setting the menus in a new and different way, and tucking ideas and tips between major items. Make the title distinctive, with come-on appeal. If a recipe takes up too much space, select a shorter one. Above all, have two or three outstanding recipes or bits of information that will make homemakers treasure the leaflet and keep it for future use.

What about art work and spots of color? By all means, if the budget permits—but keep art in proportion to copy and to size of page. A leaflet with overwhelming art work often defeats its own purpose. Encourage the artist to keep his drawings fresh, and never to underestimate the intelligence of the homemaker. Far too much art work is inclined to say, in effect, "Dishwashing is *such fun*!"

What about those so-called leaflets that come on larger size pages? Might not "Fact Sheet" or "Information Release" be a more accurate description of such material? While terminology is interesting to contemplate, it is not vital. More important is that the piece, whether 3×5 inches or $8\frac{1}{2} \times 11$ inches, be a little masterpiece of attractiveness and readability.

NEWSLETTERS PRESENT "NEWS"

As the term suggests, newsletters are usually printed on standard-sized business stationery. Sometimes the copy assumes the usual business letter format, broken up with subheads and tabulations. Sometimes it is set in two columns; sometimes it is made up like a little newspaper. The form in which copy is presented is a matter of personal (or group) opinion. The important thing to keep in mind is that every newsletter is a public relations tool. Your job is to make a good impression on your specific public.

If you are faced with editing either a professional or commercial newsletter for the first time, these 10 reminders may be helpful:

1. Remember you are dealing primarily with *News*. Examine each item with that in mind. Date your newsletter (month and year).

2. Plan to get in a variety of brief items in order to break up the pages with headlines.

3. Like the editor of a newspaper, lead off with your most important item—announcement of a forthcoming meeting or event, for example.

4. Avoid long lines of copy, long sentences, long paragraphs, and dull words!

5. If you want to group a number of short related items together in one paragraph, separate them with dots. . . .

6. If you feel the urge to inject a personal observation, box it, or set it apart from the rest of the copy to suggest that it is like an editorial.

7. Remember the old newspaper slogan, "Names make news!"

8. If you feel the need of a little art work, avoid the trite. If possible, give such art an extra

PAGE BY PAGE

Every page of a bulletin, booklet, or leaflet should present a pleasing design of type arrangement. In other words, think of it not only as a whole but also as it will appear page by page.

PHOTOGRAPHS

It's not the number of photographs that counts. It's the dramatic quality of the pictures and the way they are displayed and captioned.

dimension. Example: In an autumn newsletter that suggests falling leaves, let the leaves say something. Keep in mind that tentative, mediocre art can make serious copy appear schoolgirlish rather than professional.

CONSULT YOUR GRAMMAR!

Try to keep your points parallel when you write subheads. It isn't always possible, but it does help the booklet to march along.

9. Accept the fact that your newsletter, like the daily newspaper, is a temporary thing and not likely to be kept or filed. Therefore, if some one item is of special importance, suggest the idea of clipping it—a drawing of a pair of scissors will do it.

10. Give your newsletter a feeling of enthusiasm. How do you do this? Not by "raving," but by using lively words and expressions, and by feeling enthusiastic as you write.

Remember, however, that *all* booklets, bulletins, leaflets, newsletters, fact sheets and tear-offs do have one thing in common: They *must* look easy to read. Unless they do, your words will be wasted! It is as simple as that. ●

18.

A VISUAL APPROACH TO
Good Typography

IS IT NECESSARY for the home economist to understand type faces and technical printing terms? This is one of those questions for which no positive answer can be given. But there can be no doubt about her finding it *useful*. For, at one time or another, every home economist is concerned with the printed or mimeographed page, if to no greater extent than preparing announcements or programs for professional meetings. For the amateur, a briefing of things to do and to watch out for is in order.

If your ideas are to appear in print, try in advance to visualize them as they will look on the page.

RECOMMENDATIONS AND REMINDERS

• Develop an awareness of the looks, the design, of printed pages. Study and compare the various sizes and styles of type—not necessarily to learn their names, but to get a feeling of the relation of one to another. Study also the relation of white space to black type—much emphasis can be added by wise use of white space, and good ideas can be buried by crowding. If you are concerned with recipes, look particularly at the ways they are set in magazines, books, and leaflets. Decide what sizes and faces of type—boldface or demibold (also called heavy or medium) or italics —are, in your opinion, best for setting recipe ingredients.

• Visualize how your copy will look in finished form. Make a rough dummy in the size, shape, and number of pages of your projected circular or leaflet or whatever. Study similar publications, magazine advertisements, and other printed matter to find a sample of type that appeals to you and seems appropriate for the purpose. Cut out a few blocks of it and pin in place in your dummy. Try out some samples of headings and subheads, too. This pinup will give you a pictorial idea of how your copy might look when set in type.

TYPE SIZES

Printed recipes must be set in type that is large enough and bold enough for the homemaker to read as she works. You may have to fight to get this!

This is 6 pt.

This is 8 pt.

This is 10 pt.

This is 12 pt.

Almost any printer will give or lend you a type book to study.

• Learn to write to fit the space allowed in that dummy. To estimate roughly the number of words you can use, count the words in an average line of your pinup block of type; multiply by the number of lines in an inch; then multiply that by the approximate number of inches allotted for type. Having this number in mind, you will find yourself almost automatically turning out copy that needs little cutting or rewriting. Before typing your copy, count the characters (i.e., the number of letters and spaces) in that average line, and set your typewriter margin controls for that number of spaces. Counting your typewritten lines will tell you quickly whether or not your copy will fit the space allowed.

• Have a general idea of the type you prefer but, rather than dictate to the printer, talk it over with him. Ask his suggestions and recommendations. If you are working with an art director, he will, of course, indicate on the copy the size and face of type. You will then write to fit, according to his dictates.

• Before releasing copy, read it as a critic and shorten some of those long sentences and paragraphs, both of which make printed material look difficult to read. At the same time, avoid too many short paragraphs that end in short lines, because they tend to give the page a ragged look.

• If photographs are to be used, consider them in relation to the size they will be when reproduced. If, for example, an 8 × 10-inch photographic print must be reduced to fit a 3 × 5-inch space, you may find that the picture needs to be "cropped," eliminating needless areas. If so, it is better to mask rather than trim. Discuss this with the engraver; he may have a better answer to your problem.

PREPARING COPY TO BE MIMEOGRAPHED

Whether or not you cut your own stencils, certain procedures are essential.

• Double-space all copy so stencil cutter can follow it with ease. If you want all the finished product, or even a part of it (for emphasis), to be single-spaced, write directions for this. Double-spaced text is much easier to read, hence much more likely to be read.

Try to avoid fractions in recipes that are to be set in small type. The numeral "1/3" for example looks like "1/8" in a poorly lighted kitchen.

• Leave generous margins on your copy; if possible, have the finished product so spaced.

• Use plenty of subheads; these help the reader to get a preview of what is to come. Use variety in subheads—all capitals for the most important ones, caps and lower case for lesser ones. Other suggestions: underline all or at least the important words; place some in the center of the page, others at the left side; for those at the left, some may be set in single lines without a period, others underlined and separated from the rest of the line with a period.

When you write directions, consider the 1-2-3 approach. Makes for easy reading and following. And actually makes writing easier.

• Whenever possible, have finished product "run" (or printed) on only one side of the paper. The economy of using both sides may be negated by the difficulty encountered in reading, which may lead to its being discarded without being read.

• The long report, running as much as five to eight pages, presents a major problem in holding the reader's interest. Most important ingredient to ensure complete reading is the quality of your phrasing. Here are some mechanical devices the stencil cutter can use to avoid monotony in the format: vary the length of lines, insetting both margins for certain paragraphs; use more than one typewriter, giving diverse size and style of type; add emphasis by preceding certain paragraphs with characters available on the typewriter, such as periods, hyphens, asterisks, etc.; vary the space between paragraphs. A study of your own typewriter will suggest other possibilities.

Overcrowding is the enemy of mimeographed copy. If it runs long, either cut it or use another page.

• Keep paragraphs short and crisp.

• If it is necessary to have material printed on both sides of the sheet, choose paper heavy enough that printing will not show through.

• For the larger report you may decide to use a cover of construction paper. Here, a selection of color will add interest, may even be tied in with the theme of the report. Little would be gained by using colored paper throughout, however. Incidentally, you might consider using a typewriter with extra large type (bulletin-sized) for title, smaller type for extraneous material on the cover.

Ask for suggestions from the one who will be cutting the stencil or running off the sheets—her recommendations are likely to be most helpful. She may inspire you to step up your writing as well as to improve your format.

HEADLINE THINKING

Learn to think in headlines—short and to the point. When you do, your words will come through in type. Long, involved sentences look cluttered and vague, regardless of the type face.

MAKING CHARTS AND TABULATIONS

Graphic charts and tabulations have been called the "shorthand of statistics," and, just as shorthand is an acquired skill, so does the preparation of a complicated chart call for special know-how. In preparing simple charts, however, all you need do is to observe a few general rules such as these:

- Work first to reduce your subject matter to a headline. Until you have figured out the one big point you hope to get across and stated it in the fewest possible number of words, you are not ready to think about the form your chart might take.

- Unless you are fairly familiar with chart planning, seek help. Read up-to-date books on the subject. Study government bulletins for possibilities and variety in setups. Visit art stores where engineering supplies are sold—you will be amazed at the items which are available for giving charts an interesting look.

Clear thinking not only makes for clear writing, but it makes for a better-looking and better-reading page.

If your chart is to be reproduced in a publication, check with the editors as to kind of ink to use, heaviness of lines, and the like. Find out, too, if you can, how much your chart is likely to be reduced or enlarged. Your "Journal of Home Economics" sets forth its particular requirements in an article, "Information for Prospective Authors," January, 1965.

IT'S A GOOD IDEA . . .

To have first-hand knowledge of the various types of office copying machines. They can help you increase the efficiency and output of your department.

• Consider which direction you wish your chart to run. That is, which will give the better interpretation—perpendicular lines or horizontal ones. Use only the bars and/or lines that are needed, no more. Too many ruled lines too close together are confusing. See visuals opposite.

• Get contrast into your chart. Make some ruled lines heavier than others. Consider the possibility of adhesive-backed screens to show bars or shaded areas. Make use of color, but do not let it overpower the statistics themselves.

• Use free-hand lettering sparingly, if at all. Printed or typewritten copy, or words built with ready-made letters, give the clean-cut professional look that today's charts demand. Typewritten copy must be sharp and clear and free of erasures. In general, typewritten headings are best set in caps. Subsequent or minor heads are usually set in caps and lower case. It is usually better to do headings on separate papers, then trim to right size, and carefully tip them in place with rubber cement. Typewritten copy can be reduced 20 to 40 per cent and still be legible; a 50 per cent reduction is difficult to read.

BE CHART CONSCIOUS

The electronic age is an age of charts and tabulations. This is sure to affect the presentation of many types of written material.

• Whether you use them or not, be aware of printed symbols available for chart making—rows of little human figures to represent numbers, and the like. Incidentally, catalogs avail-

Chart Forms

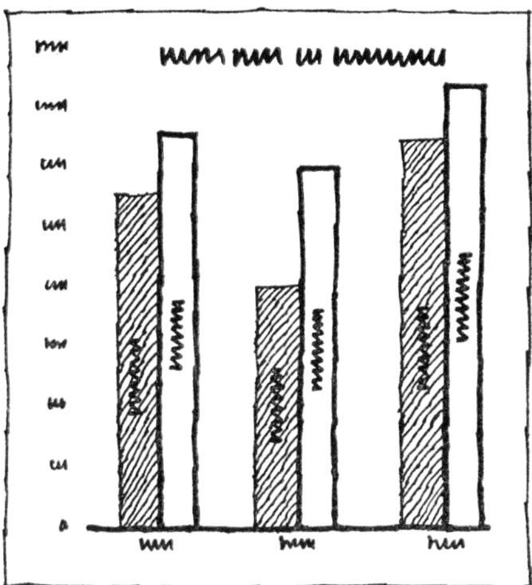

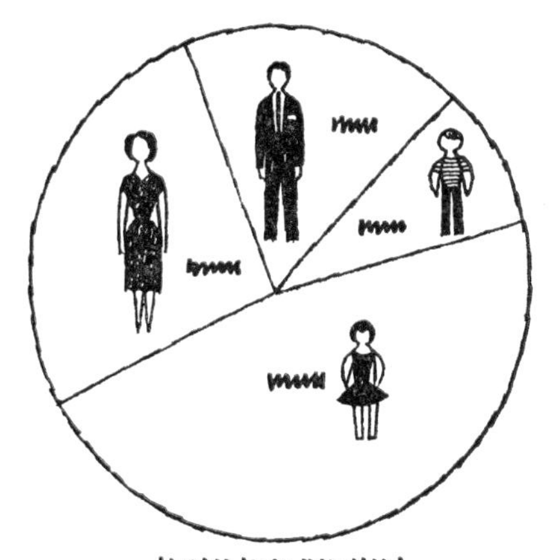

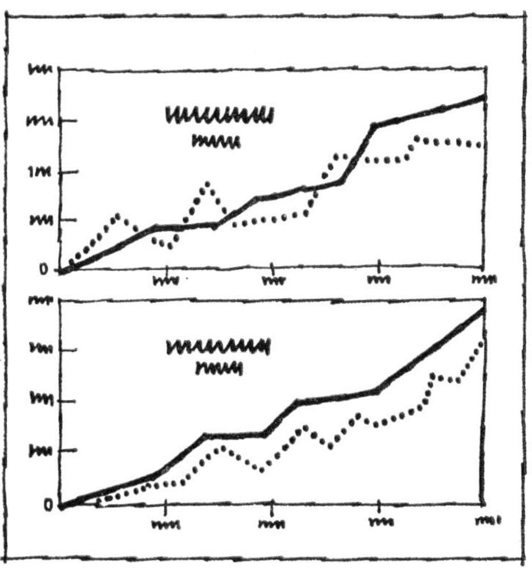

able in art supply stores show a number of symbols that are suitable for charts that have to do with homemaking information.

POINTS IN PROOFREADING

Look sharply at titles and photographic captions. Glaring errors frequently appear in the largest size type and the most conspicuous places—due partly to the fact that these are usually set by hand rather than on the machine . . . Ask someone with fresh eyes to read copy after you are "sure you have caught all the errors." He is almost certain to discover something you have missed.

OLD SAYING, REWORDED

You frequently hear someone say, "I have printer's ink in my veins." Better to say to yourself, "I am going to put red-blooded vitality into that printer's ink."

AVOID BECOMING STATIC

While there are accepted ways of setting type and setting up charts, an occasional departure from the usual is worth considering, provided it does not conflict with functionalism. For example, when you want to give a new look to a mimeographed announcement, figure how to vary the type. This is not difficult, since in most schools and departments there are various styles of typewriters available—some with script, some with oversize (i.e., bulletin) type. By shifting your sheet of paper from one machine to another you can get interesting effects.

That is, you might make the heading in bulletin type, then use script for the where-when-and-cost information, and elite type for other facts. If copy is to be reproduced by means of Xerox or Thermofax, such shifting from one machine to another is simple; a bit more difficult when you cut a stencil for mimeographed copy.

It is well to keep in mind at all times that the original concept of the word "rule" was almost synonymous with the word "law." And if a student did not obey the rules, a whack with a ruler was likely to be forthcoming! In today's thinking, however, a rule is a measure—something to go by until better rules or ways of doing are discovered or worked out. Don't be afraid to try original touches. They can help to bring your copy to life on the printed page. Which is, of course, exactly the thing you hope to achieve. ●

19.

PLANNING *Speeches* THAT WILL BE REMEMBERED

Miles of words have been written about how to plan and give a good speech. Even so, the subject calls for further exploration, especially as it relates to home economics and to showmanship. And so to analyze and explore.

As a home economist, most of your speechmaking is directed naturally to homemakers, to other home economists, to business and professional executives, to students, or others concerned directly or indirectly with home economics.

Since your talks to homemakers about homemaking usually take the form of demonstrations or show-and-tell presentations, showmanship is less of a problem, because action or illustrative materials help to supply that needed element. When, however, your talk is dependent entirely on words and how you use them, dramatization is more difficult.

Ask yourself not only what you would like to say, but what the audience might like to hear.

One way to get around the problem is to think of your talk in terms of a play, with four or five acts. In Act 1, Scene 1 (the very opening of your speech) you set the stage for what is to follow, just as the playwright does. You create a mental picture and establish a mood, after which you develop your points—your "acts." This is how it works out.

SET THE STAGE AND PRESENT A WORD PICTURE

Situation. You are a home economics supervisor speaking at a joint meeting of home economics teachers and business home economists. Your aim is to get across how you use or might use business-sponsored teaching aids in your school system. You begin by giving a word picture of your city and its schools, number of home economics departments, number of teachers, types of students, and the general direction of your courses in homemaking. Along with setting the scene, you make the audience aware of your responsibility as a supervisor; help everyone to understand the scope of your problems as they relate to visual aids.

Folk singer Bob Dylan was asked how he had put in his day and he said, "I was creatin' and crematin'." A more prosaic person would have said, "I was writing, but burned up most of what I wrote."

After this preliminary picture, you then go on to outline in one-two-three fashion what types of wall charts, filmstrips, and the like you can best use. You do not, of course, merely state those points; you round them out with case histories, concrete examples, and personal observations that keep the speech moving.

It's the way you put words together that counts. Ten women can wear the same type of hat. On some it looks ordinary; on others it becomes high style.

Situation. You are a business home economist speaking to a group of students on Career Day. Your assignment is to tell something about your job that will be of interest to those young people. In setting this scene you describe your department and what goes on in it. You state the aim of or reason for your department—i.e., to be of genuine help to homemakers and thereby help to build their interest in your company's products.

You tell, perhaps, some of your struggles in getting your position.

You do not, however, build your entire talk around yourself and your work. Instead, you go on to explain what type of training is needed or desirable for the various tasks which you and your co-workers must perform. You give some idea of the scope of opportunities in positions like your own. You make three or four specific points—and there is your talk, neatly tied together.

Good speeches are like sandwiches—they need plenty of meat, with a little buttering up. A bit of "ham" is good; so is a bit of wry!

Situation. You are giving an annual report of work done by a committee of which you are chairman. Even though the report is a brief one, you begin with a quick description of your committee personnel; you outline the aims of your project, and state the one big thing you accomplished during the year. You then break your report down into two or three parts in which you give some of the side effects of your achievements. And you frequently sign it off with a light touch, as did the home demonstration agent who ended one report by saying, "Incidentally, while achieving these results, I attended 24 potluck luncheons and dinners, and ate three gallons of spaghetti and four gallons of potato salad!"

COMPARISONS BRING STATEMENTS TO LIFE

Have you ever listened to a talk that appeared to be well organized and well delivered, but did not quite come through to the audience? Usually this is a sign that the speaker did not take the necessary time and thought to expand important statements. To illustrate: A nutrition specialist speaking before a luncheon group was describing the work of her national committee in planning foods for flights into outer space. She

5 DON'TS

One well-known speaker offers these "don'ts."

1. Don't sound egotistical.
2. Don't mention your lack of preparation. (The audience can tell!)
3. Don't try to be funny. And don't be funny unless it fits.
4. Don't talk over the heads of or down to the audience. Talk directly to the people in it.
5. Don't be afraid of idealism, just so it isn't preaching.

said, "For this flight, all of the food for two men on a 4-day (or longer) flight had to fit into a space of not more than 4,000 cubic inches."

This figure meant little to those in the audience. But she went on to say, "How much is 4,000 cubic inches? Well, that's about the size of an ordinary suitcase 20 inches long, 20 inches wide, and 10 inches deep." Then everyone in the group visualized those 4,000 cubic inches and had much clearer understanding of the problem.

This method of comparing or contrasting one thing with another is one of the oldest and most effective devices in teaching or speaking (or writing). Beginning with the parables in the Bible, any number of speeches have been built entirely on analogy. One such example was a talk given a number of years ago entitled "The Eggbeater and I" which traced the parallel history of home economics in business with the history of the eggbeater from fork to modern electric beater, and with the professional history of the speaker. Certainly there was nothing profound about that approach, but it was a peg on which to hang an interesting talk. (Another such example is related in the authors' note at the end of Chapter 15.)

ABOUT STAGE FRIGHT

A certain amount of stage fright is natural. If you do not have some emotional tension, chances are you will not induce emotional contagion.

TO READ OR NOT TO READ

Every speaker must do what is natural. If you feel more assured reading your speech, read it—but read it well. If you find it easy to speak from notes or from memory, do it. Be yourself!

IT'S A GOOD IDEA

- In planning any speech it is a good idea to take enough time to think out a provocative title. Not one that will merely attract attention, but that suggests the summation of what you hope to get across. Once you have such a title it becomes your topic sentence, and the points to be developed fall into line naturally.

- After you have thought through what you want to say, and have outlined your points—

first mentally, then on paper—it is well to go ahead and write out the talk much as you plan to give it. It is then comparatively easy to edit and tighten it for publication—which is usually a requirement for any major speech.

• It is always a good idea to create a kind of mental timer which will enable you to speed up or slow down your comments, dependent on time. And always have a definite sign-off line in mind, so that if time is running out you can end your talk quickly on a succinct statement or thought, rather than to fumble hurriedly and feebly for words.

• When you are to be interviewed on radio or television, or to take part in a panel discussion, it is a good idea to think out in advance one or two important statements and be ready to state them briefly but clearly. In a way, an interview is really a foreshortened speech which must have studied meaning, yet give the impression of being spontaneous.

Consider using a spotlight to emphasize visuals when making a talk. It is a courtesy to your audience, and it helps to dramatize the visuals.

• If, in your work, you are likely to be called on frequently for informal talks, it is well to build toward such possibilities. While on a trip to a foreign country, for example, you might make notes on some one feature of your trip, as food, or clothing, or houses, or flower arrangement—something connected with your vocation or avocation. Your notes can then be quickly pulled together for a particular occasion. One extension clothing specialist made it a point to collect an article of clothing from every country she visited: quaint lace caps from Normandy, mantillas from Spain, sailors' bright blue pants from Holland, and so on. With such a display, she was always equipped to give an interesting illustrated talk.

COURTESY

We all know that it is discourteous to force a speaker to sit through a long period of preliminaries. If you, the speaker, have this happen to you, spend that time figuring how to shorten your speech accordingly.

There are, of course, no absolute rules that apply under all circumstances, but one thing is certain—the more showmanship you put into any talk, the greater the remembership! Perhaps it is just a single thought or idea, or an interesting case history, or a likening of one thing to another that helps the meaning to come through and be retained. But unless something you say is remembered, your words have been in vain.

WHAT ABOUT TELEVISION?

If you are concerned with educational television—as a planner, writer, or performer—you have, perhaps, observed that much of the information in this book is adaptable to that form of communication. For television, as it relates to home-centered programs, is a combination of lively demonstration and skillful use of visual materials, plus a talent for teaching and a flair for unselfconscious showmanship.

At the time this book is being written, a top television personality is Julia Child, the "French Chef" of the National Educational Network, whose show has been picked up by practically every educational station across the country. What is behind Mrs. Child's wide and enthusiastic following? The answer is simple. She has, in addition to a thorough knowledge of French cookery, an abundance of cooking skills at her fingertips which she demonstrates with good-humored informality, without stiffness or slickness. She has her audience literally "eating out of her hand."

According to a feature story in the *Des Moines Register*, Mrs. Child's television career began when she was interviewed over a local station, discussing publication of the book *Mastering the Art of French Cooking* which she coau-

LIGHTING

Before the meeting is set up, study the lighting of the room, if possible. Glaring lights in the front of the room are unflattering to the speaker—and often put the audience to sleep!

thored with two Paris colleagues. During the course of the interview she was shown stirring up a French omelet, chattering away as if in her own kitchen. Response was so immediate and so favorable that she was signed to do a series on cooking which, with subsequent series, was eventually released all over the country.

These facts are stated here to stress the importance of genuine showmanship in all televised presentations, and to remind you that every speech or interview, wherever or whenever given, can be of vast importance in the development of your career.

TEST

One test of a speech is whether or not there is anything in it worth quoting. Reporters always look for this. It helps to say something quotable in the first two minutes.

20.

PUTTING SHOWMANSHIP INTO *Professional Programs*

IT IS ONE THING to say that professional meetings should be more dynamic; that greater showmanship should be injected into programs. The doing is not so simple—as well you know, if you have ever served on a program committee.

While there are no ready-made answers to the problem, the ideas and quotes that follow may prove helpful to you.

THINK BIG—THINK NEW

It all adds up to this: Plan a lively, interesting program, then "keep the show on the road."

Some of your programs may not live up to your expectations; others may turn out to be spectacular. In some instances you may find your big idea unworkable, but it is the starting place for your planning. One home economist interviewed contends that the word "new" should be the basis of every program. What it means to put a *new* food product on the market, for example. How the *newer* fabrics are dictating new sewing and laundering techniques. A *new* look at multiple housing—its advantages and disadvantages. And so on.

See if the combination of thinking big and thinking new does not automatically suggest possible subjects, possible speakers, possible ways to dramatize a program or series of programs.

HAVE A PLAN BUT KEEP IT FLEXIBLE

The program committee's first task is to block out the year's programs. It is, of course, wise to do this. But beware of too rigid planning! Instead of following the it-has-always-been-done-this-way pattern, ask yourselves such questions as these:

- Is there any reason why each year there must be a joint meeting of business home economists, teachers, and dietitians?

- Would it be better to have such a get-together every two years and make it a special "little convention" meeting?

- Is it always advisable to have each member identify herself in every meeting?

- Might not the chairman make a sort of group introduction occasionally?

- Is it necessary to have an outside speaker at every meeting?

- Might it not be more refreshing to have an occasional panel discussion by members of the organization?

- And, for a small group, why not a meeting built around "Share and Tell"? In this program each member brings a new product, or an illustra-

FOR FUN

Ask every member to bring one or more artificial flowers to build an instant arrangement for the speaker's table. After the meeting, the flowers can go to a retirement or convalescent home.

For an informal luncheon meeting, have each one bring a sandwich for a "sandwich swap." With the 'wiches, serve chewy relishes and hot consommé plus dessert and coffee.

tion on which she has worked, or an artifact from another part of the world, or even a new type of hat that can be made in 10 minutes, with an added minute or two to discuss her offering!

Regardless of your decisions, do try to keep your programs from being static. It is one big step toward achieving showmanship.

GIFT PROJECT

One HEIB group schedules its do-for-others project the week before Easter rather than at Christmas time. Avoids duplication of what other groups are doing.

BRING OUT THE BEST IN YOUR SPEAKERS

Do you agree that, in general, it is well to select speakers who have an interest in—or at least an understanding of—home economics? When speaker and audience think on the same beam, audience participation is automatic. And such participation is a vital part of showmanship.

Usually it is better to decide upon a subject before approaching a speaker. For example, you decide that your business or dietetics group would be interested in and profit by a discussion as to how home economics is changing in our schools. Once you have arrived at a choice of subject matter, it is not difficult to find a local home economics supervisor who will talk informally and helpfully.

In approaching any outside speaker, give him or her a clear word picture of the group and the type of talk preferred. Discuss possible titles with him, working all the time for one that will not only attract attention, but will help to keep the speaker in the groove. For some of the meetings select a speaker from within the organization itself, giving her a definite assignment—perhaps to interview all of the newspaper food editors of the community as to the questions they are most frequently asked, or the type of material most acceptable to them.

CAREER DAY FAIR

Has your group ever staged a Career Fair? A city-wide or county-wide meeting with demonstration booths, food, entertainment, etc. makes an exciting event. Students from various schools can get acquainted with one another and with working home economists in various fields.

Doing such leg-and-brain work and then reporting on it helps to develop good speakers as well as good programs, and suggests to others in the group that it pays to have an inquiring mind.

HAVE A GOOD M.C. OR MODERATOR

One thing is certain: there cannot be showmanship unless there is a showman. In any program the one in charge (whether she be the chairman of the group, the chairman of the program committee, or an experienced mistress of ceremonies) must have or must develop the ability to keep the meeting on the move, to inject genuine enthusiasm into it, to make it informal as well as professional.

One chairman goes so far as to contend that informality is the secret of showmanship. At the beginning of a meeting she may ask, for example, "Well, how many of you vacationed in Europe this summer?" Or, "Mary, have you eaten in any especially interesting restaurants lately?" Or, "Betty, what, in your opinion, was the outstanding talk given at the national convention?" Two or three minutes of such spontaneous ice breaking is frequently of more value than the main event itself.

TV TALK

For a program that is interesting and helpful, build it around how to be interviewed on TV. Get a local commentator to help show how and how not to speak into a microphone; how to prepare for an interview; how to dress; how to look friendly and natural. Make it an audience participation show, by all means.

BUILD UP ANTICIPATION FOR THE PROGRAM

The place to start in generating enthusiasm for a meeting is in the announcement. It is not enough to state simply when and where the meeting will take place, how much the dinner will cost, and who is to be the speaker. Clothe that skeleton announcement with a few picture-making words, as: "Dinner ($5.50 including tip) will be served in the beautiful new Crystal Room, with Chef Oscar promising us his special Cherries Jubilee

DOCUMENTARY

Would it be feasible for your group to plan a documentary film on Home Economics? One that goes into history, yet reports the present and looks to the future. If it can be made to mean something to the general public, a sponsor is almost certain to be forthcoming.

for dessert." Or, "We are fortunate in having Mrs. Wallace Brown as our speaker. Her experiences in teaching home economics in the mountain areas of Peru are interesting, exciting, and eye opening."

TOASTMASTER TOUCH

Invite someone from the local Toastmistress Club to pass along some of the things she has learned. Makes an interesting talk; acquaints members with what such a club can do to improve one's public speaking.

DIVIDE THE RESPONSIBILITY

One key that opens the door to group enthusiasm lies in making every member feel a part of every program. To achieve this the chairman may, at the beginning of the year, urge all members to inform the chairman as to possible subjects, possible speakers, and possible projects that might be undertaken. In addition, she may occasionally telephone a member of the group to ask, "How did you think the program went over last night?" Or, "Have you any suggestions as to what we might do to build up our treasury at the next meeting?" Calling on various persons for help has a double advantage: it makes those persons more interested in the organization itself, and it takes some of the burden off the hard-working Executive Board members.

SUGGESTIONS

At a fall meeting have half a dozen high school boys and girls (not all A students!) report on their vacation jobs, and what they learned . . . Plan a program by and about working mothers (not all perfectionists) and how their problems relate to home economics. A good interviewer is important.

In brief, Program Showmanship can be summed up in three words: *anticipation* (for what the meeting promises); *emancipation* (freedom from old ways of doing); and *participation* (by the audience). Keep these uppermost in your mind as you plan those programs and put them into action. See if your meetings are not more dramatic and dynamic.

And your rewards can be summed up in two phrases: *better attended*, and *better remembered.* ●

21.

SPECIAL PROBLEMS OF

Business Home Economists

WHY DO SO MANY new-on-the-job home economists find it difficult to make the progress they had hoped for? Why does an occasional business home economist remain unhappily static in her job for too long a time; or merely mark time when she might be going ahead? Why is it that some of us, even after working for many years, never quite achieve the goals we have set for ourselves?

There are hundreds of possible answers to these and similar questions. But in the seasoned judgment of business executives, there are three main reasons for difficulties on the job. They are:

Lack of writing skills
Lack of imagination and daring
A seeming lack of executive ability, or a hesitancy to assume and/or delegate responsibility

Unless you are able to state and analyze your problem, you really do have one!

Any one of these shortcomings can hold one back. And any one of them can be conquered, if the troubled home economist recognizes her difficulties and works to overcome them.

Let's consider each problem, and what can be done about it.

WRITE YOUR WAY TO ADVANCEMENT

If you are a one-woman home economics department in a business firm, or a member of a small, all-purpose home economics staff, your writing falls into two general classifications. And, to some extent, the same holds true in a large department where each home economist has her own specific duties to perform.

First, there is the "paper work"—those memos, reports, and the like that go directly to the boss. Visualize him or her. Remember that he would not be an executive unless he had developed the ability to think clearly and to get to the point quickly. Your cue is to proceed as he does. In all interoffice communications figure out the main thought you want to get across and state it in the first paragraph. If possible in the first sentence. Leave no doubt as to what your piece of writing is about. Which is, of course, just another way of saying, "Until you have reduced your thinking to a topic sentence, you are not ready to write anything." Least of all something as important as those reports and presentations.

Second, you will probably have to plan and write various types of informational material for the homemaking public. This may include writing copy for everything from leaflets or booklets to directions for use and/or care of products for food cartons, fabric hang-tags, or instruction books for equipment. It may involve writing information releases for newspapers. All of which calls for everything you have or can develop in the way of writing skills.

WHY LAST?

Since this chapter can mean much to young home economists, why is it placed at the end of this book, rather than near the beginning? So that teachers and department heads can turn to it quickly, then turn it over to students or new employees.

In such writing you visualize those homemakers who will, you hope, eventually read and profit by what you have written. You do not, however, bypass the possible reactions of your immediate superior, even though he does not insist on seeing everything that you write. After you have put your material into finished form (and not before) ask for his opinion and guidance. Be grateful for it. His judgment may well be better than yours, for he is looking at your copy in relation to other and bigger problems. Incidentally, he knows quite a lot about homemakers. After all, he is probably married to one!

SUCCESS STORY

One advertising executive attributes a large part of her success to the advice given by a graduation speaker: "Don't die on third base!"

THINK FRESH AND FAR OUT, BUT KEEP ON THE BEAM OF PRACTICALITY

What does that word "creativity" really mean?

An outstanding philosopher, interviewed on television, expressed it something like this: *"In its original definition, creation meant making something out of nothing. In today's usage, it means making something that has not previously existed, though it is made of things that are already in existence."*

In that sense, one may speak of "creating" a new food product such as a completely new packaged mix; a revolutionary type of cooking equipment; another in a series of amazing new fabrics. Technologists are constantly at work "creating" this sort of thing.

HALF TRUTH

Is it true that writing is a form of self-expression? Not entirely. In how-to-do-it writing, "self" is of little or no importance. Emphasis must always be on subject matter and on the reader.

Only the poet can afford the luxury of saying what he really feels without regard to audience reaction.

In our home economics world, we can claim some degree of creativity when we design a hat, or think up a new way of using something that the technologists have brought into being. We can consider ourselves creative when we work out a really new recipe—but scarcely so when we merely substitute orange extract for vanilla in a cake recipe, or add dill weed to a salad dressing. The recipe merry-go-round is loaded with that limited type of creativity.

Getting Down to Cases

Question is, how do you go about developing greater creativity? Biggest stimulus is the need to answer a specific problem. And the answer comes not from inspiration but from concentration. Let's take a fairly typical situation.

You are a not-too-experienced home economist working for a firm that specializes in publicizing and promoting food products. Your assignment is to come up with new recipes for dry lima beans which will "upgrade them socially," forgetting the old "wash-day dinner" type of approach. (That is an interesting and sensible point of view, you recognize, for wash day and wash-day dinners have gone the way of the washboard.)

AUTHORS' NOTE ON AUTHORITY

Every home economist is an authority in her work. A few are authorities in unusual areas of the job. Example: One who works for a sugar company has expanded her specialty beyond sugar cookery—she has developed skill and renown for her table decorations made with sweets. Most famous are her sugar bells.

After making certain your basic directions for cooking those limas are sound, up to date, and as simple as you can make them, your first step is to make a quick survey of current cookbooks, recipe booklets, magazines, and newspaper columns. No, you are not looking for recipes which you might adapt—you just want to get an idea of how many and what kind of recipes calling for lima beans are being published.

Next, you do some intensive thinking as to what types of recipes seem to be *lacking*. You visualize the great variety and popularity of herbs and spices and seasonings available in every market; new products in frozen and canned forms. You visualize the young women you see in those markets, and you ask yourself what types of lima recipes would appeal most to these alert young homemakers. And you decide that probably appetizers and salads, and buffet or barbeque-type casseroles with meat or cheese and modern seasonings would head the list.

Thus fortified, you proceed to talk to yourself, something like this:

I wonder what would happen if I put cooked limas into the blender, along with cheese or deviled ham, to make a dip in which the limas would extend the higher priced items. I wonder if anyone has ever worked out a kind of Caesar salad using limas, one crunchy with toasted garlic croutons, and perhaps with snippets of salami instead of the usual anchovies. I wonder how a Lima Bean Vichyssoise would be. Or something that might be called "Limas Rumanoff," a new type of casserole laced with rum. And so on through a long list of what-might-be-dones.

Some of your brainstorms, you find, have real possibilities which you proceed to develop. Others you cross off the list quickly. Now it is time to toss your thinking into the ring for others of the staff to discuss, judge, add to, and take from. Your plans will be challenged and changed. For that is the way of business.

Ideas Beget Ideas

One interesting facet of creative thinking is that the more you do of it, the more ideas you have. Never be afraid to reach far out. You (or someone else) can always bring your dreams down to practicality. And will.

DEFINITION

Creativity is not thinking up an idea. It is thinking through a problem and figuring out an unexpected solution to it.

Can you overdo fresh thinking? Not if you keep within the boundaries of good taste, true helpfulness, and the policies of your company. It is true that a creative person can sometimes become so wrapped up in her own creations that she loses sight temporarily of the over-all aims of a department or organization. However, as one executive puts it, *"It's always a lot easier to slow down a person who is too full of ideas than it is to steam up someone who has too few."*

PROVE THAT YOU HAVE EXECUTIVE ABILITY

If you are secure in the feeling that your thinking is objective and that you can produce sound ideas with original touches, you will speak, act, and write with a certain degree of authority. However, you may need to accentuate that quality. And you may very well need to remind the executives in your company that you have it!

IT WORKS TWO WAYS

If you hope to be in the executive class, learn to delegate responsibility as well as accept it—*expect* and *demand,* if necessary, good work from your secretary and others under your jurisdiction.

How do you remind those executives? One way is to use visuals. That is, when you have a suggestion or a recommendation to present, put it into visual form rather than talk about it. If it is an idea for a new recipe that will stimulate sales of the company's products, make up the dish for your immediate boss—and others—to sample. If you have a concept of a new layout for a photograph or a display, show in a sketch what you have in mind. If you want to sell a plan of action, ask permission to outline your thinking in written form. And in all such presentations, show quietly that you are thinking at executive level.

Show, too, by your actions and procedures that you are working to develop the Five Business Senses, which are:

- *A sense of the significant.* (Some call it judgment.) More than one businessman considers this the most important attribute any employee could have. It shows up in all planning and creative work—in all decisions—in all relations with the public. Well, let's just say that it shows up in everything!

- *A sense of timing.* In show business,

timing is tremendously important to the success of an act. This is equally true in business. We have to sense when is the best time to spring a new idea on the boss or the public. We have to style our material to fit the times.

• *A sense of proportion*, which is another way of saying a sense of humor. That means the ability to laugh at oneself and at annoyances. (A noted publisher used to remark, "*Remember, everything is relatively unimportant!*") Every one of us needs to work hard to cultivate this saving sense. To keep in mind that while a wife can get away with temperament at home, a home economist in business cannot.

• *Financial sense or sales sense.* This, to a home economist, means seeing the connection between the work she is doing in a test kitchen or a photographer's studio or on the typewriter and the promotion of sales of the products with which she is concerned. That connection may be direct or indirect, but it must be there.

ABOUT DICTATION

Know what you intend to say before you start to dictate. But dictate. Most executives do.

• *A sense of the dramatic.* Not primadonnaism, but the vision to present the problems of homemaking from a dramatic angle. Writing, photographs, presentations, demonstrations—everything we do—dare not be done in a dull, boring, obvious way; it should be done with the dramatic lift which has been stressed throughout this book.

WORDS

Work to show that you not only have skills and ability, but that you have "ideability."

SPECIFIC PROBLEMS COMMON TO CERTAIN JOB CATEGORIES

Situation. You are a recent graduate working in the lower echelons of the home economics department of a large company. Your problem is to fit yourself and your capabilities into that organization and to do it quickly, which means a complete switch-over from college life to a life of business. You find that you must learn to test and write recipes according to a pattern that differs from the standard way you were taught to write them. You also discover that detailed records are more important than you had thought them to be.

Being young and eager, you are alive with ideas. You wonder whether or not to take them up with the head of your department.

Part of good showmanship lies in "let-go-manship." The old pro worries in advance, but when he gets on the golf course or the stage, he relaxes—lets go. If he could not do this, he would not have become a pro!

The answer is "yes." If your timing is right, and your attitude modest and objective, you and your ideas will receive a good hearing. And by such discussions you learn why some of your suggestions are good, why others are unworkable, and how to improve them. Thus, little by little, you become a business home economist.

Situation. You have been working for several years in the same job. Your responsibilities have been multiplying at a rapid rate. You do not have the time or the energy to think through new programs and put them into motion. What do you do about it?

One solution is to decide whether you are best and happiest as a creative person or as an administrator. (You may find it advisable to have an objective-minded friend help you to make this decision, or at least listen while you come to a conclusion for yourself, before discussing it with your employer.) If you are primarily creative, you may decide to ask for help in reorganizing your department in order to free you from some detail.

If, however, you or your employer feels that you are best as an administrator, you must not be disappointed if the creative side of your job is turned over to a food stylist (who may or may not be a home economist) or to the creative department of some outside agency. Business is a many-sided thing. At times you may need to "choose up sides" mentally, in order to see in what direction you can make the most progress for yourself and your organization.

Situation. After working for a number of years, you may consider becoming a free-lance home economist or a consultant. (And there is a big difference between the two!)

Here your basic problem lies in your ability to face reality. Unless you can answer most of the following questions affirmatively, you are not ready for the big step.

1. Are you, or is your name, fairly well known?
2. Do you have wide contacts, and know how to make new ones?
3. Have you a specialty or some set of skills that makes you particularly valuable? (A deftness in handling food in photography, for example.)
4. Are you able to translate your ideas and findings into a form that your client will readily grasp and understand? In other words, do you know how to put out a professional looking report or sales presentation?
5. Have you resources (or a husband!) that will pay a good part of your overhead, especially while you are getting started?
6. Are you willing to work harder and longer than would be necessary in a Monday-to-Friday position?

PUBLIC RELATIONS

Be a one-woman public relations ambassador for your company, both inside and outside the organization. This helps build you up toward the executive level. And more—it helps you *enjoy* your work!

If you can measure up to these problems, you probably will be able to master the many others that are certain to arise.

BACK TO SHOWMANSHIP

Whatever your job category, whatever your capabilities and skills, never underestimate the importance of worthwhile ideas. Show that you can produce them. Show that you have the necessary showmanship to put them into action.

Is good showmanship a gift that one must be born with? No. Although some fortunate persons are endowed naturally with a certain flair, most of us must acquire it by years of serious study, trials and errors, failures and successes, and just plain hard work.

SIGN OFF

Be grateful that you can use imagination in your work. Relatively few persons are so fortunate.

Beware, however, of airing your seriousness and determination. Beware of visible stress and strain. After you have put your all into behind-the-scenes planning, relax. Then proceed to speak or write or act with the quiet assurance that is always the mark of the true professional. ●

Descriptive Index